TELEVISION IN AMERICA

A PICTORIAL HISTORY

First published in U.S.A. in 1986
by Exeter Books
Distributed by Bookthrift
Exeter is a trademark of Bookthrift Marketing, Inc.
Bookthrift is a registered trademark of Bookthrift Marketing, Inc.
New York, New York

ISBN 0-671-08195-0

Printed in Belgium

Below left: Taxi - starring Judd Hirsch and Marilu Henner.
Below right: Barney Miller, starring Hal Linden
Bottom right: The Cartwrights of **Bonanza** - Lorne Greene, Michael Landon, Dan Blocker and Pernell Roberts.
Opposite right: Barbara Walters interviews George Burns.
Opposite left: Adam West as the Caped Crusader and Burt Ward as The Boy Wonder in **Batman**.

TELEVISION IN AMERICA
A PICTORIAL HISTORY
THOMAS G AYLESWORTH

Exeter Books

NEW YORK

A Bison Book

For my daughter Carol

Without whose help, especially with the soaps, this book would have taken twice as long to write. As Oscar Hammerstein II put it in Carousel: 'My little girl is half again as bright as girls are meant to be.'

Sid Caesar and Imogene Coca were the stars of **Your Show of Shows**.

CONTENTS

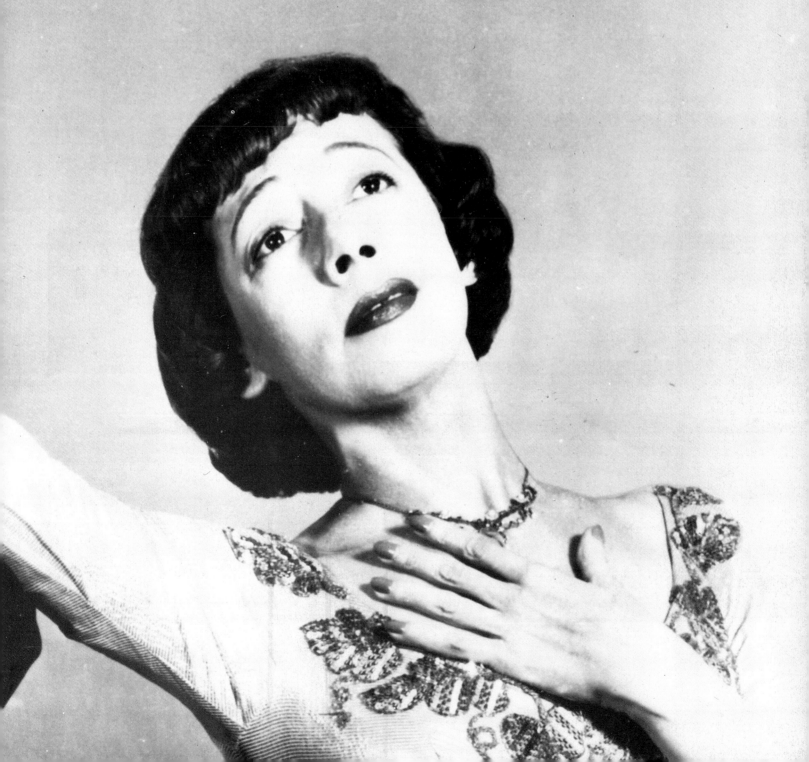

Top left: Ed Asner played the crusading editor in **Lou Grant**.
Top right: Philip Michael Thomas (as Detective Tubbs, left) and Don Johnson (as Detective Crockett) on **Miami Vice**.

Bottom left: Phil Silvers was Master Sergeant Ernie Bilko on **The Phil Silvers Show** (aka **You'll Never Get Rich**).
Bottom right: The first walk on the moon—Neil A Armstrong, 1969.

Opposite: Milton Berle was surely 'The King of Comedy.'

PREFACE

Contrary to popular opinion, Milton Berle was not 'Mr Television' when the first American televised transmission began in 1931. Actually, he was a mere stripling—barely 22 years old. It was on 30 July 1930 that the Radio Corporation of America and its subsidiary, the National Broadcasting Company, began operating an experimental station, W2XBS, in New York City. The station introduced kinescope receivers in 1931. The Columbia Broadcasting System started a regular schedule of telecasting on station W2XAB in New York City on 21 July 1933, which continued until 23 February 1933. On 30 April 1939, just as the New York World's Fair was opened, the first regular commercial television broadcasts were begun in New York City. Then television production was discontinued during World War II.

In 1946, after the war, television began to burst up on the American scene with a speed unforeseen even by the most optimistic leaders of the industry. The novelty of seeing TV pictures in the home caught the public's fancy and began a revolution in the world of entertainment. Not that there was much to look at at first. Of course, local stations in all parts of the country had their own programs—limited as they might be. But as for network schedules, entertainment had to be awaited with bated breath, and remember that not all stations were on the network, and most of those that were had to wait for the kinescope films to arrive from New York, Chicago or Los Angeles.

In 1946, network television looked like this: Sunday, **Western Movie** (8-9 PM, Eastern time, Dumont); **Face to Face, Geographically Speaking, Television Screen Magazine** (8-9, NBC). Monday, **Esso Newsreel, Voice of Firestone Televues** (7:45-8:15 PM, NBC) and **Gillette Cavalcade of Sports** (9-11 PM,NBC). Tuesday, **Play the Game** (8-8:30 PM, Dumont) and **Serving Through Science** (9-9:30 PM, Dumont). Wednesday, **Faraway Hill** (9-9:30 PM, Dumont). Thursday, **Cash and Carry** (9-9:30 PM, Dumont) and **Esso Newsreel, Hourglass** and **Fight Film Filler** (7:45-9:15 PM, NBC). Friday, **You Are an Artist, I Love to Eat** and **The World in Your Home** (8:15-9 PM,NBC) and **Gillette Cavalcade of Sports** (9:30-11 PM, NBC). Saturday, nothing. ABC and CBS were not in the running that year, and few of these programs would seem today to be things that people would stay home to watch. But they did.

Nineteen forty-seven was not much better, although some of the programs started at 7 PM and there were such important new entries as the **Kraft Television Theatre**. Still, ABC and CBS were not on the air with network programs, and NBC was the only entry on Sundays; Dumont had things all to themselves on Tuesdays, and Saturday was still dark. Then came 1948, and the dam had burst. There were four networks, and every day of the week, television could be viewed from 7 to 11 PM. Most of it was trash, but several TV milestones started that year—**Studio One, Toast of the Town** (with Ed Sullivan), **Philco Playhouse, Arthur Godfrey's Talent Scouts, America's Town Meeting of the Air, We, the People, Texaco Star Theater** (with Milton Berle) and **Face the Music**.

The American public had a new love—television—a love that has continued unabated ever since. Of course, we are fickle. We have lusted for and then rejected many different types of programming—variety shows, adult Westerns, swinging detectives, idiot situation comedies, kids sitcoms, relevant shows, fantasy shows, soap operas, escapist shows, sci-fi shows and God love us, weirdies like **The Gong Show** and **Real People**. We are fickle, but we know that these types of shows will come back and, no matter what, we remain true to our main love—television.

VARIETY SHOWS

In the early days of television, when he had to shell out $400 or more for a set with a four-inch screen, what the average TV viewer wanted was a lot of action for his money—and that meant variety shows. One of the first, and most fondly remembered, of these programs that were soon to be called 'vaudeo shows'—a combination of vaudeville and video—was the **Texaco Star Theater** with Milton Berle.

Uncle Miltie was TV's first superstar and lasted from 1948 to 1956 with his slapstick, crazy costumes and sight gags. His chief competition in the variety show game was, of course Ed Sullivan, the inept emcee of **The Toast of the Town** (later **The Ed Sullivan Show**), with his weekly melange of comedians, country singers, pop singers, opera singers, acrobats, puppets and dancing bears.

There was also **The All Star Revue** with Jimmy Durante, **Your Show of Shows** with Sid Caesar and Imogene Coca, **The Colgate Comedy Hour** with, at various times, Eddie Cantor, Martin and Lewis, Abbott and Costello and Bob Hope, plus scores more of lesser importance. But their appeal died in the late 1950s.

Above: Sid Caesar often played the role of Professor von Wolfgang—the authority on almost everything—on **Your Show of Shows**, the 90-minute NBC Saturday night fixture from 1950 to 1954. Imogene Coca, Carl Reiner and Howard Morris helped.

Below: The venerable comedian from Indiana—Red Skelton (who prefers to be known as a clown)—starred in **The Red Skelton Show** for 20 years, 1951 to 1971. A gentle, warm, human funny man, his signoff was a sincere 'God bless.'

Left: Skelton playing his role as Freddie the Freeloader, the hobo who never spoke. Among the other characters he played on his show were The Mean Widdle Kid, Clem Kadiddlehopper, Sheriff Deadeye, Cauliflower McPugg, Willie Lump-Lump and Bolivar Shagnasty.

Opposite: Two of the most beloved of all the television comedians—George Burns (left) and Jack Benny. **The George Burns and Gracie Allen Show** was a hit for eight years, 1950 to 1958, when Gracie retired. **The Jack Benny Show** was a must-see for 15 years.

Opposite top: Steve Lawrence and Eydie Gorme are among the most pleasant and durable of all the variety show singers. Lawrence got his start on TV in 1950 on **Arthur Godfrey's Talent Scouts**, he teamed with Gorme on the short-lived **Guide Right** show in 1952 and later on Steve Allen's **Tonight** show, it was 'the start of something big.'

Opposite bottom: The Sonny and Cher Comedy Hour ran on CBS from 1971 to 1977 and featured the then-married Sonny Bono and Cher. Their theme was Bono's song 'The Beat Goes On,' and they sang, they acted, they clowned. Along the way, they gave a leg up to such newcomers as Steve Martin, Shields and Yarnell and Teri Garr.

Below: Perry Como began in television in 1948 on **The Chesterfield Supper Club**, which was merely a simulcast of his popular radio show. Singing his theme song, 'Dream Along With Me (I'm on My Way to a Star),' Como won over his fans with his easygoing crooning and relaxed delivery. In 1950 he starred in **The Perry Como Show**, a three-a-week 15-minute program. He hit the big time in 1955 with an hour-long prime time variety show, which lasted for eight years. Since 1963 he has confined himself to specials.

Right: Bob Hope (here with one of his guest stars, the Pink Panther) made his television debut on **The Ed Sullivan Show**, then went on to become one of the emcees of **Chesterfield Sound Off Time** (1951) and **The Colgate Comedy Hour** (1952). Since that time he has never been off the TV screen for too long and his Christmas Specials are seen by millions.

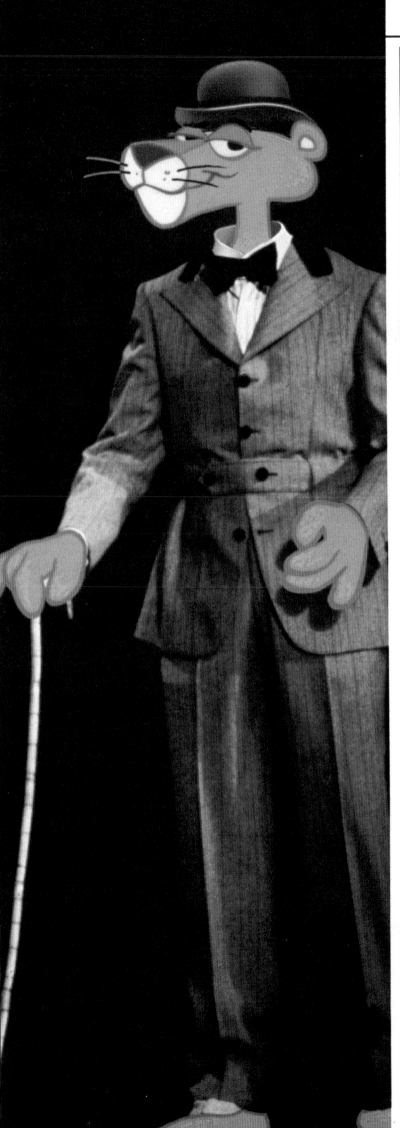

Left: The perennial teenager, Dick Clark, whose **American Bandstand** began as a local show in Philadelphia in 1952. The format was the same when he moved to a network show in 1957—a couple of performers would lip-synch their current pop hits and chat with Clark. The rest of the show was devoted to listening to current hit records and watching an army of teenagers dance to them.

Opposite: Donnie and Marie, starring the Osmonds, was a musical variety show that ran on ABC for four years from 1976 to 1979. Donnie was 18 and Marie was 16 when it premiered.

Above: Band leader Lawrence Welk was the star of **The Lawrence Welk Show**, which was a fixture on ABC's Saturday night schedule from 1963 to 1971. Then the network felt that the program's audience was confined to the older generation and cancelled the show. Welk went into syndication and stayed on the air from 1971 to 1982 for a 19-year total run. The show featured good, old-fashioned melodic music and everything was good, clean and wholesome. The fans went wild at 'The Champagne Music of Lawrence Welk,' the bubble machine, the theme songs ('Bubbles in the Wine' and later 'Champagne Fanfare'). Who cared that Welk had about at much stage presence as Ed Sullivan? When he played the accordian or danced the polka with a lady from the audience, his followers were enchanted.

Left: Julian Lennon as a video jockey on Music Television—MTV—on cable.

Opposite: NBC's Saturday Night Live began its long run on 11 October 1975. Here, from the original cast, are Garrett Morris and Laraine Newman (bottom steps), John Belushi (top steps), Chevy Chase (left), Gilda Radner (standing on steps) and Jane Curtin and Dan Aykroyd (right)—the 'Not Ready for Prime Time Players.'
Below: 'The Great White North' segment from the **SCTV Network** show. The segment was presented as a talk show for beer-drinking Canadian hunters and featured Rick Moranis (left) and Dave Thomas as Bob and Doug MacKenzie. These shows, produced in Canada, were expansions of the old **Second City TV** syndicated series.

Above: Elliott Gould, while serving as guest host on **NBC's Saturday Night Live**, played an electrician confronted by the Coneheads, aliens from the planet Remulak. Left to right, daughter Connie (Laraine Newman), Gould, Primat (Jane Curtin) and Beldar (Dan Ackroyd).

Right: Two of televisions most beloved funny people—Carol Burnett and Bill Cosby, both of whom have had their own comedy shows. Burnett has won two Emmy Awards from The National Academy of Television Arts and Sciences, and Cosby has won three.

Right: Dan Rowan (left) and Dick Martin created a new type of variety show in their **Rowan and Martin's Laugh-In**, which ran on NBC on Monday nights from 1968 to 1973. It combined black-outs, sketches, one-liners and cameo appearances by celebrities. Out of the whole thing came such catch-phrases as 'Sock it to me,' 'You bet your bippy,' 'Verrry Interesting,' 'Look that up your your Funk and Wagnalls,' 'Beautiful downtown Burbank' and 'Here come de judge.' Getting their first big break were such cast members as Ruth Buzzi, Judy Carne, Goldie Hawn, Arte Johnson, Henry Gibson, Jo Anne Worley, Lily Tomlin and Richard Dawson. The pace never let up.

Left: Steve Allen (top right) is the star of the Disney Channel's **Steve Allen's Comedy Room**. Here he hosts comedians Billy Crystal, Milton Berle and Carl Reiner (front row, L to R) and Joe Baker and Dale Gonyea (top row, L to R).
Opposite: Tom (left) and Dick Smothers—the stars of **The Smothers Brothers Comedy Hour**, which bounced around on all three networks from 1967 to 1970 and reappeared in 1975. Tom was the dumb half of the comedy/singing team, and Dick was the sensible one.

Left: Elliot Reid (left) and Henry Morgan were regulars on **That Was the Week That Was** (or **TW 3**) when it premiered in 1964. The program was a first—a comedy political satire operation, and it was presented live.

Left: Johnny Carson, costumed as the host of one of his skits, 'The Art Fern Tea Time Movie' on **The Tonight Show**. With him is Carol Wayne as the 'Matinee Lady.' The unflappable Carson has been holding down the job of host on this program since 1962 and shows no sign of flagging. Among his other skits on the show have been 'Stump the Band' where members of the audience give titles of obscure songs and ask Doc Severinsen and the boys to play the tunes; 'Carnac the Magnificent' with Carson as an inept magician; 'The Mighty Carson Art Players,' usually a movie spoof; 'Aunt Blabby'; 'Carswell' in which Carson is a psychic predicting the future; 'Faharishi,' in which he is a yogi; 'Floyd R Turbo,' in which he is a superpatriot; and 'Father Time.' In addition to these sketches, the show contains an opening topical comedy monologue and a great deal of talking to visiting celebrities.

Above: Johnny Carson talking with one of his guests—Robert Mitchum—on **The Tonight Show**.

Left: Jack Paar was the host of **The Tonight Show** from 1957 to 1962, having taken the job over from Steve Allen and Ernie Kovacs. Paar was at his best during the interview segments, being incisive, witty and emotional. Among his regular stable of ranconteurs were Hugh Downs, Dody Goodman, Tedi Thurman and Jose Melis. Semi-regulars included Elsa Maxwell, Genevieve, Cliff Arquette (as Charley Weaver), Pat Harrington Jr (as Guido Panzini), Hans Conreid, Peggy Cass, Alexander King, Joey Bishop, Hermione Gingold, Florence Henderson, Buddy Hackett and Betty White. He also did sketches, and probably the most popular was 'What Is It?' Paar would show the audience some strange-looking object and then explain what it was used for. This has also been done by Johnny Carson.

Above: Berle, pretending to be a trombonist in a skit with stage and screen comic star Victor Moore in April 1949.

Left: Berle still had time to mug as a guest star on **The Jack Benny Show.**

Right: Berle celebrates Washington's birthday.

Far right: One of Berle's many drag skits—as Elizabeth Taylor in **Cleopatra.**

Milton Berle won the job of star of **The Texaco Star Theater** over stiff competition—Harry Richman, Georgie Price, Henny Youngman, Morey Amsterdam, Jack Carter and Peter Donald also rotated in the host's spot. After three months of this game of musical emcees, Berle was given the nod in September 1948. He proceeded to become 'Mr Television.'

Jackie Gleason started out on the old Dumont Network with **The Cavalcade of Stars**, but was lured away by CBS (with a whopping pay increase—from $1600 to $8000 per week) and began **The Jackie Gleason Show** in 1952—it lasted off and on for 18 years.
Right: One of Gleason's characters was The Poor Soul, who never spoke yet was always in embarrassing situations.
Below: Gleason before the cameras after his monologue, saying, 'And away we go!'
Far right: Gleason as Reggie Van Gleason III, a blase, incredibly rich tippler, who got rid of his limousines when their ashtrays were full.

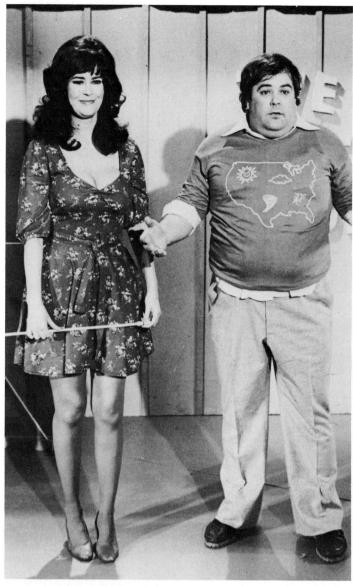

Above: The Flip Wilson Show ran on NBC from 1970 to 1974, and Wilson was the first black performer to achieve major popularity as host of his own variety hour. He used music and guests, but his own comedy skits were the highlight of the program. Here Wilson plays 'Jeraldine Jones'; a sassy swinging, liberated woman with a boy friend named 'Killer.'

Right: Hee Haw was a sort of country **Rowan and Martin's Laugh-In** with Western and Gospel music. It ran on CBS from 1969 to 1971, and then went into syndication. Here are two of the stars, Gailard Sartain and Lisa Todd. Other stalwarts were Roy Clark, Buck Owens, Grandpa Jones, Stringbean, Sheb Wooley, Minnie Pearl, Roy Acuff and John Henry Faulk.

Left: Steve Allen would put up with a lot on his television shows, whether it was on **The Tonight Show, The Steve Allen Comedy Hour,** or **The Steve Allen Show**.
Opposite: Left to right, Vickie Lawrence, Tim Conway and Carol Burnett on **The Carol Burnett Show**, which ran for 12 years on CBS—from 1967 to 1979. Carol Burnett was the glue that held the show together She could sing, dance, act, clown and mime with the best of them. Still, she had a whole raft of second bananas and the chemistry among them was outstanding. In addition to Lawrence and Conway, there were Harvey Korman, Lyle Waggoner, Dick Van Dyke, Craig Richard Nelson, Ken Berry and Steve Lawrence. CBS didn't want to let Burnett go and edited the comedy sketches from the original show into half-hour; segments, syndicating them as **Carol Burnett and Friends**. They are still running.

VARIETY SHOWS

Right: Fran Tarkenton (left) and Cathy Lee Crosby were two of the three hosts on **That's Incredible!**, which ran on ABC from 1980 to 1984. The other host was singer John Davidson. Tarkenton had been a star quarterback for the Minnesota Vikings and the New York Giants of the National Football League, and was amiable. Crosby and Davidson were happy show-biz types. But they were all given pretty poor material on this show. It was a freak show, featuring film clips of such things as a man juggling whirring chain saws, a skydiver falling through the air while handcuffed and straitjacketed, a man jumping over cars speeding at him at a mile a minute or a group of karate experts knocking down a barn. The program was voted 'Most Sadistic Show' by **Time** Magazine in 1980.

Above: The original weirdo show, after which **That's Incredible!** was patterned, was **Real People**. Shown are some of the regulars: Bill Rafferty (top), Byron Allen, Sarah Purcell, Skip Stephenson,(center row) and John Barbour. Other regulars included Fred Willard, Mark Russel, Kerry Millerick and Peter Billingsley. The show was the brainchild of George Schlatter, who produced **Laugh-In**.

Opposite far right: David Letterman, whose **Late Night with David Letterman** premiered in 1982 and took the night owl crowd by storm. The master of the non-interview, Letterman specializes in zany features, such as his 'Stupid Pet Tricks' feature in which animal owners appear with their pets to demonstrate nonsensical tricks that they have taught the animals. He once let a woman in the audience take over the show.

Right: Allen Funt (right) with announcer Durward Kirby on **Candid Camera**, which ran from 1948 to 1950 and returned in 1953 and again in 1960. By using hidden cameras, Funt would chronicle the reactions of everyday people situations. For example, he once had singer Dorothy Collins (formerly on **Your Hit Parade** coast her car down a hill into a service station. She complained to the attendent that the car wouldn't start and when he looked under the hood there was no engine there. Funt arranged for waitresses in restaurants to serve unbelievably small portions to diners. He had a young lady stand on the sidewalk with two large suitcases and ask a passing man to help her carry them. She then picked one up (it was empty) and the man picked up the other—or rather tried to, since it was filled with 200 pounds of concrete.

For years, Ed Sullivan had been a newspaper man in New York, most famous for writing a gossip column. Then he was tapped to be the host on a new program that CBS was developing, The show was to be called **You're the Top**, but that was overruled and **Toast of the Town** was substituted. The show eventually became, of course, **The Ed Sullivan Show**, and it lasted for 24 years, from 1948 to 1971. lt was truly a variety show. Appearing on the same night might be an operatic soprano, a rock star, a chorus line, a comedian, a ballet and a recitation from a Broadway play. No one minded that Sullivan had no stage presence (his voice, mispronunciations and stiff mannerisms were widely imitated by professional impressionists), he knew how to ferret out talent and put on a good show.

Right: Ed Sullivan in his prime. His first program on 20 June 1948 had a budget of only $1375, and only $375 of that was allocated for the performers. The guest stars of the show were Dean Martin and Jerry Lewis, and they took home $200 of that. Also on that premiere show were pianist Eugene List, Richard Rodgers and Oscar Hammerstein II and the six original June Taylor Dancers (called 'The Toastettes').

Below: Count Basie, (right), the great band leader, appearing with Sullivan on **The Ed Sullivan Show,** Many entertainers and other personalities made their American television debuts on the program—Charles Laughton, Bon Hope, Lena Horne, Dean Martin, Jerry Lewis, Dinah Shore, Eddie Fisher, the Beatles and even Walt Disney—for example. The appearance of Elvis Presley in 1956 (not his debut, by the way) made headlines.

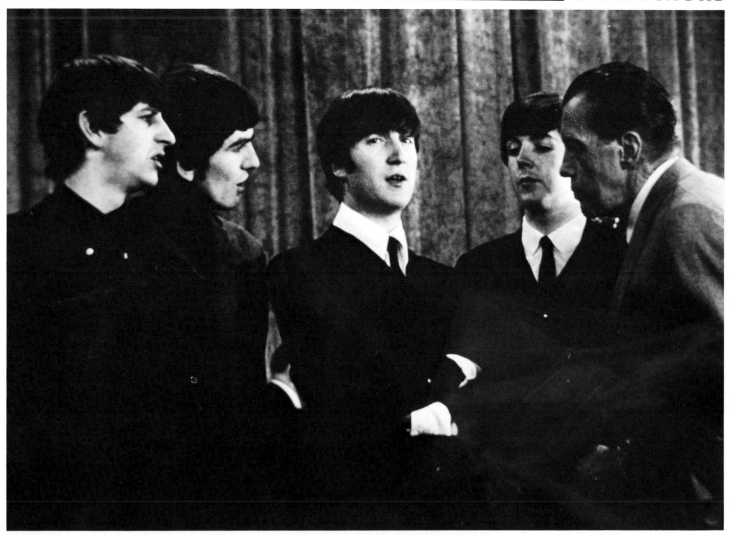

Above: In 1963 Sullivan brought that Liverpudlian quartet, The Beatles, over from England to appear on his show, and they were sensational. All over the country young female rock 'n' roll fans were fainting on their living room floor. Left to right: Ringo Starr, George Harrison, John Lennon, Paul McCartney and Ed Sullivan. **Left:** Sullivan's television appearances were not confined to **The Ed Sullivan Show**. Here he is shown with two award winners in his second appearance as the host of **Ed Sullivan Presents: The Second Annual Entertainer of the Year Awards** on 14 January 1972. On the left is Carol Burnett, who was in her fifth year of starring in the incredibly successful **The Carol Burnett Show**, and on the right is Jean Stapleton, who was in her second year of playing Edith 'Dingbat' Bunker on **All in the Family**—a comedic masterpiece. Sullivan also appeared in the movie **Bye Bye Birdie** (1963), playing himself, of course.

SITUATION COMEDIES

Situation comedies have been likened to human comic strips, and they tend to be small hunks of life exaggerated for comic purposes. There have been sitcoms about families (**I Love Lucy**), spies (**Get Smart!**), the occult (**Bewitched**), the US Army (**The Phil Silvers Show**) Navy (**Hennessey**) and Marines (**Gomer Pyle, USMC**), rustics (**The Beverly Hillbillies**) and sophisticates (**Benson**), ethnics (**The Goldbergs**) and even war itself (**M*A*S*H**). Every area of human endeavor is fair game, and about the only things that the various sitcoms have in common is their ubiquitous laugh tracks. Sitcoms were in at the beginning of TV in America. In 1949 could be seen **The Goldbergs** (with Gertrude Berg), **Mama** (with Peggy Wood), **The Aldrich Family, Apartment 3-C, The Hartmans** (with Paul and Grace Hartman), **Heavens to Betsy, The Life of Riley** (with Jackie Gleason), **Lum and Abner, Wesley, Wren's Nest** and **Young and Gay**.

Left: Late in the five-year run (1959-1963) of **The Many Loves of Dobie Gillis**, the teen-age sitcom, Dobie and his best friend, Maynard G Krebs (played by Bob Denver, right), were drafted. Here the dopey Krebs talks with guest star Jim Backus.
Above: Gertrude Berg in **The Goldbergs**. She also wrote the show, and did commercials for Sanka.
Opposite: The cast of **Topper**—Marion and George Kerby (Anne Jeffries and Robert Sterling, standing), Cosmo and Henrietta Topper (Leo G Carroll and Lee Patrick), and Neil the dog.

Above left: George Burns and Gracie Allen of **The George Burns and Gracie Allen Show,** which ran from 1950 to 1958 on CBS. George had a dual role: he was both the on-screen narrator of the zany proceedings and straight man for Gracie's lovable scatterbrained involvements with a variety of people.
Left: The cast of **Petticoat Junction**—standing: Edgar Buchanan and Bea Benaderet (as Uncle Joe Carson and Kate Bradley); sitting: Jeannine Riley, Pat Woodell and Linda Kaye (as Kate's daughters, Billie Jo, Bobbie Jo and Betty Jo). This rural sitcom was set in the small farming community of Hooterville, where Kate ran the Shady Rest Hotel, Uncle Joe had assumed the title of manager of the establishment.

Above: Danny Thomas (left) casts a questioning look at his television prodigies Annette Funicello (the former Mouseketeer, who played Gina Minelli, an Italian exchange student living with the Williamses) and Richard Tyler (as Buck, Gina's boyfriend), on **The Danny Thomas Show**, aka **Make Room for Daddy**, which ran from 1953 to 1965 and reappeared from 1970 to 1971.

Right: The cast of the second version of **The Life of Riley**, which ran from 1953 to 1958: Marjorie Reynolds and William Bendix (seated) played Peg and Chester A Riley; Lugene Sanders and Wesley Morgan (standing) played their children, Babs and Junior. Previously (1949 - 1950), Jackie Gleason and Rosemary DeCamp were Chester and Peg.

Left: One of the idiotic confrontations in the Campbell family (Richard Mulligan, Ted Wass and Cathryn Damon), that could be seen every week on **Soap**, which ran from 1977 to 1981 on ABC.

Below left: Henry Winkler (right), played Arthur 'Fonzie' Fonzarelli in **Happy Days,** the long-running (1974-1984) teen sitcom on ABC. Originally, The Fonz was a minor character in the series, but Winkler was so good as the motorcycle-riding high school dropout that he moved from fifth billing to third, then to second, and finally to first when Ron Howard (Richie Cunningham) left in 1980.

Opposite: Joyce DeWitt and John Ritter in **Three's Company.** a *menage a trois* sitcom that ran from 1977 to 1984 on ABC. The premise was that two single girls (the other was Suzanne Somers) needed a roommate to help with the expenses, and they end up with Ritter.

Below: Mortal enemies Gretchen Kraus (played by Inga Swenson) and Benson DuBois (Robert Guillaume) are tied up on **Benson**.

SITUATION COMEDIES

No television star has endured as long as the beloved and irrepressible comic genius Lucille Ball. She became the toast of television in 1951 in **I Love Lucy**, a show that was to run for 10 years. She switched from being Lucy Ricardo to being Lucy Carmichael on **The Lucy Show** in 1962. This one ran for 12 years, although both the name of the show **(Here's Lucy)** and the name of the star (Lucille Carter) were changed in 1968. Along the way there were such spinoffs as **The Lucy-Desi Comedy Hour** (1962-1967) and **Lucy in Connecticut** (the summer of 1960). Today, reruns of these shows can be seen on television at all times and at all hours. It was the great comedienne herself who said, 'I loved playing Lucy Ricardo—I got to act out all my childhood fantasies.' This darling of three generations of television viewers should surely be declared a national treasure.

Below: A typical scene from the long-running **I Love Lucy** show. The men are overwhelmed while the women are blithely ignorant of the fact that something has gone wrong. Left to right: Desi Arnaz, William Frawley, Vivian Vance, Lucille Ball, playinq, respectively, Ricky Ricardo, Fred Mertz (or 'Frat Mers,' as Ricky would call him in his Cuban accent), Ethel Mertz and Lucy Ricardo. The success of this program is unparalleled in the history of television.

Right: Desiderio Alberto Arnaz III and his wife, Lucille Ball, on the set of the **I Love Lucy** show. They decided at the beginning to form their own company, Desilu, to handle the the show, and it was a wise move, since they decided to do the program on film. This meant that they could broadcast a clearer picture than the kinescopes in use at the time, and they would also own the vast library of films of the show to use in syndication.

Above: Somehow Lucille Ball managed to get a pie in the face of one of her guest stars while he was trying to order lunch in a restaurant. Then came the classic line, 'Oh, gosh, Ethel—it's William Holden!'

Right: Lucille Ball and guest star Chuck Connors rehearse for the 'Lucy and Chuck Connors Have a Surprise Slumber Party' episode on **Here's Lucy**. Lucy is not aware that her home has been rented to a movie company for $200 per day. Connors, at the end of a day of shooting, decides to sleep in the house rather than drive 50 miles back home. Lucy also comes home late to get some sleep. As she crawls into bed she discovers Connors. Not knowing who he is, she breaks a lamp over his head, knocking him unconscious. Finally realizing who he is, she tries to prop him up so that he will think he has had a bad dream. But he comes to in time to discover her little plot. Though sporting a sore head, Connors leaves Lucy, gladly, but not before planting a huge kiss on Her cheek. Corny? Sure. But also hilarious.

Above: The cast of **Family Affair**: Sebastian Cabot (as Mr Giles French, the English gentleman's gentleman, top left), Johnny Whitaker (Jody), Brian Keith (Bill Davis), Kathy Garver (Cissy) and Anissa Jones (Buffy, front) holding Mrs Beazley, her doll. The show, which ran from 1966 to 1971, told the story of a swinging bachelor who suddenly has to bring up his dead brother's three orphaned children.

Left: Lisa Bonet plays Denise Huxtable and Bill Cosby plays Dr Heathcliff (Cliff) Huxtable, her father, on the successful **The Cosby Show**, which premiered in 1984.

Above left: Isabel Sanford, as Louise Jefferson, played opposite Sherman Hemsley, as George Jefferson, in **The Jeffersons**, a spinoff of **All In The Family**, which premiered in 1975.

Opposite: The **Hazel** cast—clockwise: Bobby Buntrock, Ray Fulmer, Shirley Booth, Julia Benjamin, Lynn Borden.

Left: All in the Family premiered in 1971 and ran for 12 years. Pictured are the four characters who made the show what it was—the number one show in the nation for its first five years—seated: Jean Stapleton (as Edith 'Dingbat' Bunker), Carroll O'Connor (as Archie Bunker); standing: Rob Reiner (as Mike 'Meathead' Stivic), Sally Struthers (as Gloria Bunker Stivic). This was the program that changed the course of television sitcom history, bringing reality to the tube, complete with bigotry, racial epithets and offensive characters. Archie was a working-class Joe who hated everyone who was not white, Protestant and Anglo-Saxon, while his son-in-law, Mike, was a liberal college student. Archie's biggest problem, however, was that he seemed to be unable to escape the people he was prejudiced against. He had to work with a racially mixed group of people. A black family, the Jeffersons, lived next door. His son-in-law was a Polish-American. He eventually had to take in a Puerto Rican boarder. It sounded depressing, but actually the producer, Norman Lear, was able to create an extremely funny show. Archie always lost the argument, but the program held up a mirror to the audience and made them look at it

Left: Dick Van Dyke was Rob Petrie, a television comedy writer, and Mary Tyler Moore was his wife, Laura, on **The Dick Van Dyke Show**, which ran from 1961 to 1966 on CBS. The program masterminded by Carl Reiner, was one of the classic sitcoms of all time because of its excellent scripts and first-class cast, which also included Rose Marie, Morey Amsterdam, Larry Mathews, Richard Deacon, Jerry Paris, Ann Morgan Guilbert and, occasionally playing Alan Brady, the variety show comedian for who Van Dyke, Rose Marie and Amsterdam write, Carl Reiner himself. It took three seasons for the program to become a hit, but it was still in the top twenty when it left the air.

Below: Top Row: Donna Reed (Donna Stone) and Paul Peterson (Jeff Stone). Seated: Patty Peterson (Trisha Stone) and Carl Betz (Dr Alex Stone). These were four-fifths of the Stone family on **The Donna Reed Show**, which ran from 1958 to 1966 on ABC. The missing member of the family was Shelley Fabares, who played daughter Mary. The problems on the show were pretty typically family sitcom ones—measles, girl friends, school problems, little white lies, Alex's late night house calls.

Opposite below left: Little Lauren Chapin (as Kathy 'Kitten' Anderson) hands her mother an Easter egg as the rest of her family looks on— Billy Gray (James 'Bud' Anderson Jr), Elinor Donahue (Betty 'Princess' Anderson), Jane Wyatt (Margaret Anderson) and Robert Young (Jim Anderson)—in **Father Knows Best**, the classic wholesome family sitcom that ran from 1955 to 1963.

Opposite below right: Another wholesome family sitcom is **Family Ties**, which premiered in 1982. Left to right: Michael J Fox (as Alex), Michael Gross (Steven), Meredith Baxter-Birney (Elyse), Tina Yothers (Jennifer) and Justine Bateman (Mallory)— The Keaton family. While it is as squeaky clean as **Father Knows Best**, it also confronts contemporary issues.

M★A★S★H was something completely different—a comedy about war. Probably at any other time in the nation's history, such a program would not have worked. But in 1972, when the series premiered, the United States was embroiled in the lingering war in Vietnam. The climate created by this unpopular conflict made it seem right to tell the story of the 4077th Mobile Army Surgical Hospital. Of course it was set in a different war—the Korean conflict in the early 1950s—but the setting could just as easily have been Vietnam. The doctors were depressed by the futility of patching up a soldier only to have him sent back to the front lines, the horrible living conditions in the field, and the general insanity of the war. Naturally, the only thing they could do was laugh. This truly was the first sitcom to use black humor. And few episodes went by without a scene in the operating room—just to bring home the reality of war. CBS threatened to cancel the show during its first year, but cooler heads prevailed, and the show got a second chance the next year, happily sandwiched between **All in the Family** and **The Mary Tyler Moore Show**. It was a hit and lasted for 11 years until 1983, ending with a two and one-half hour special show.

Above: Captains 'Trapper' John McIntyre (Wayne Rogers) and Benjamin Franklin 'Hawkeye' Pierce (Alan Alda) are handcuffed as Lieutenant Colonel Henry Blake (McLean Stevenson) approves.
Right: Colonel Sherman Potter (Harry Morgan), the veteran surgeon of three wars, surveys the devastation.
Opposite top: 'Hawkeye' Pierce is noncommittal as Major Charles Emerson Winchester (David Ogden Stiers), Corporal Maxwell Klinger (Jamie Farr) and Father John Mulcahey (William Christopher) are overcome with either pride or patriotism.
Opposite bottom: One of the few refuges that Hawkeye (Alan Alda) had in the craziness of the war was the shower. It was Alda who held the **M*A*S*H** troupe together.

Above: Colonel Wilhelm Klink (Werner Klemperer) checks out the weapon of Colonel Robert Hogan (Bob Crane) on **Hogan's Heroes**, a war sitcom that ran from 1965 to 1971. Hogan was the leader of the prisoners in Stalag 13, a German prisoner of war camp, and Klink the commandant of the prison. This was not **M*A*S*H**, but tried to make the point that being a prisoner of war could be fun. The camp contained a French chef, a steam room, a barber shop and more comforts than that at home. Besides, weren't the Germans all bumbling nincompoops?

Right: A casual stranger is mystified by Maxwell Smart's shoephone in **Get Smart!** which ran from 1965 to 1970, starring Don Adams as Smart—Agent 86. He worked for the US intelligence agency CONTROL, and was an inept version of James Bond as he battled the evil agents of KAOS along with his brilliant and beautiful partner, Agent 99 (Barbara Feldon) and their boss, Thaddeus, the Chief (Edward Platt). This program gave the youth of America 'Would you believe?'

Above: Phil Silvers (as Sergeant Ernie Bilko, center) is trapped by Colonel John T Hall (Paul Ford, right) as Private Dino Paparelli (Billy Sands) looks on in **The Phil Silvers Show**. This hilarious comedy about an army con-man ran from 1955 to 1959 on CBS and is still in syndication.
Right: Car 54, Where Are You? was created by Nat Hiken, the matermind behind **The Phil Silvers Show**, and starred Joe E Ross (left, who had appeared with Silvers as Mess Sergeant Rupert Ritzik) as Patrolman Gunther Toody and Fred Gwynn as Patrolman Francis Muldoon. Toody was short, stocky, friendly, nosy and not too bright. Muldoon was tall, quiet, and easily bored. The slapstick series, which premiered in 1961, was shot on location in The Bronx. It was a good thing that the show was shot in black and white, because the Car 54 in question was painted red and white so passersby would not mistake it for a real NYPD car. It was a great show, stuck somewhere between the Keystone Kops and **Barney Miller**, but was cancelled after a mere two seasons.

Above: Frank Sutton (top) played Sergeant Vince Carter and Jim Nabors was Private Gomer Pyle on **Gomer Pyle, USMC**, which was a spinoff of **The Andy Griffith Show** in which Pyle's bumbling, naive, likable rural character was transferred to a Marine boot camp. Carter was always confounded by Gomer's innocence and trust. The show ran on CBS from 1964 to 1969, returning for the summer of 1970.

Above right: Sally Field as Sister Bertrille in **The Flying Nun**, which ran from 1967 to 1970 on ABC. She was a young novice, who brightened lives at the Convent San Tanco in Puerto Rico. She weighed a mere 90 pounds, and could fly when a stiff wind caught her starched cornette.

Right: Andy Griffith (right) played Sheriff Andy Taylor on **The Andy Griffith Show,** which ran from 1960 to 1968. With him is the young Ron Howard (as his son, Opie), who was to go on to **Happy Days** and a life as a fine film director. The program was the best of the homespun comedies.

Left: The staff of Mel's Diner in Phoenix—from **Alice**, which premiered in 1976. Left to right: Polly Holliday (as Florence Jean 'Flo' Castleberry), Beth Howland (as Vera Louise Gorman), Linda Lavin (as Alice Hyatt) and Vic Tayback (as Mel Sharples). The series was based on the movie **Alice Doesn't Live Here Anymore** (1974). Lavin did well with the title role, for which Ellen Burstyn had won an Academy Award.

Below: Hal Linden (left) in the title role of **Barney Miller**, a hilarious and yet accurate police sitcom which ran from 1975 to 1982. With him is Ron Carey, as the sycophantic Officer Carl Levitt. Captain Miller was the leader of a motley crew of detectives in a dilapidated station house in New York.

Below right: Left to right: Tony Danza (as Tony Banta), Judd Hirsch (as Alex Rieger), Jeff Conaway (as Bobby Wheeler) and Marilu Henner (as Elaine Nardo)—the drivers in **Taxi**, the story of New York's Sunshine Cab Company. Despite critical acclaim for the ensemble acting, the wit and charm of the writing and the faith of its fans, **Taxi** lasted only three years (1980-1983).

Below: Ted Lange (left) played bartender Isaac Washington on **The Love Boat**, which premiered in 1977 on ABC. Seen with him is one of the many guest stars, the former professional football standout Roosevelt Grier, who, it turns out, would rather cook than play a tough guy.

Since the beginning of television in the United States there have been young people on the tube during prime time, although they were often attached to a family in which the parents were the main characters. Molly and Jake Goldberg (Getrude Berg and Philip Loeb) had their Rosalie and Sammy (Arlene McQuade and Larry Robinson) on **The Goldbergs** in 1949. In that same year, Marta and Lars Hansen (Peggy Wood and Judson Laire) had their Katrin, Dagmar and Nels (Rosemary Rice, Robin Morgan and Dick Van Patten—yes, Dick Van Patten) on **Mama**. Two other shows featured youngsters in 1949. **The Aldrich Family** starred Robert Casey as Henry Aldrich and House Jameson and Lois Wilson as his parents. **The Life of Riley** starred Jackie Gleason as Chester A Riley and Rosemary DeCamp as his wife, Peg, with Lanny Rees and Gloria Winters as their two kids, Junior and Babs. So out of the 12 shows that debuted in that maiden year of sitcoms, one starred a youngster and three featured kids. Gradually the situation comedies starring children began to proliferate. **Meet Corliss Archer** (starring Lugene Sanders) premiered in 1950. In 1951 there was **A Date with Judy** (Patricia Crowley) and **Young Mr Bobbin** (Jackie Kelk). By 1960 it seemed as if the kids had taken over the tube. There were **Dennis the Menace, The Many Loves of Dobie Gillis**, and **Leave it to Beaver** to watch. At present there are rafts of kid sitcoms. **Silver Spoons, Punky Brewster, Charles in Charge, Family Ties, Webster, Diff'rent Strokes, The Facts of Life** are all carried by the kid stars.

Right: Arnold (Gary Coleman, left) is set to demonstate his martial arts skill to his brother Willis (Todd Bridges) in the 'Return of the Gooch' episode on NBC's **Diff'rent Strokes.** The premise of the show is that eight-year-old Arnold and 12-year-old Willis are two Harlem boys who are adopted by the millionaire Philip Drummond (Conrad Bain), who had employed their now-dead mother as a housekeeper. The comedy arose when the ghetto-reared kids try to cope with the wealthy atmosphere in the Drummond household.
Above right: Jay North (left) played Dennis Mitchell and Joseph Kearns was his long suffering neighbor, George Wilson, in **Dennis the Menace**, which ran from 1959 to 1963. Dennis went through life donating Mr Wilson's rare coins to the March of Dimes, digging up Mr Wilson's flowers and planting potatoes, and so on, making life miserable for one and all.
Opposite: Jerry Mathers (left) was Theodore 'Beaver' Cleaver and Tony Dow was his older brother Wally in **Leave it to Beaver**, which ran from 1958 to 1963 and remains a cult program to this day in reruns. Beaver was a typical kid, more interested in frogs than girls, but Wally was just entering puberty. Hugh Beaumont and Barbara Billingsley were the parents.

Left: Stuffy Mrs Margaret Drysdale (Harriet MacGibbon,) the wife of wealthy banker Milburn Drysdale, can't stand the thought of sampling the corn squeezin's of Daisy 'Granny' Moses (Irene Ryan). Granny's son-in-law, Jed Clampett (Buddy Ebsen) is at right. **The Beverly Hillbillies** ran on CBS from 1962 to 1971 and told the story of the attempts of a newly-rich rustic family to adjust to life in the fast lane. Also in the cast were Donna Douglas as Elly May Clampett and Max Baer Jr as Jethro Bodine. Sample lines: 'Do you like Kipling?' 'I don't know—I ain't never kippled.'
Below left: Green Acres, which ran from 1965 to 1971, was a spinoff from **Petticoat Junction**, which, in turn, was a spinoff from **The Beverly Hillbillies**, Eva Gabor was Lisa Douglas and Eddie Albert was her husband, Oliver Wendell Douglas. The plot revolved around Oliver, who had been an extremely successful New York lawyer, and his obsession with getting back to the soil. He buys a run-down farm near Hooterville, and moves his city-loving wife to hillbilly country. The program and its two predecessors were canceled in the celebrated 1971 'hick show' purge by CBS.
Below: Left to right: Cloris Leachman as Phyllis Lindstrom, Mary Tyler Moore as Mary Richards and Valerie Harper as Rhoda Morgenstern on **The Mary Tyler Moore Show**, which was the most stylish sitcom on the air from 1970 to 1977. In those seven years the show won 25 Emmys. Others in the cast included Ed Asner as Lou Grant, the producer, Ted Knight as Ted Baxter, the anchorman, Gavin MacLeod as Murray Slaughter, the newswriter and Betty White as Sue Ann Nivens, the Happy Homemaker of WJM-TV.

Above: A smug Ralph Kramden (Jackie Gleason) does not impress his wife, Alice (Audrey Meadows), as upstairs neighbors Ed and Trixie Norton (Art Carney and Joyce Randolph) look on. **The Honeymooners**, which began as a skit on **The Jackie Gleason Show**, went on its own from 1955 to 1956, and was revived in 1971 with Gleason, Carney, Sheila MacRae (as Alice) and Jane Kean (as Trixie). One of the things that made this different from the usual sitcom was that the four didn't live in neat little suburban homes, but rather in a grimy run-down apartment building in Brooklyn. Ralph was not the suave, good-looking, upper middle class hero; he was fat, blustery, avaricious, and a loser. Ralph was a bus driver and his best friend, Norton, was a rather incompetent, slow-witted sewer worker. The show, now in reruns, built up a cult following; the 'honeymoonies' can watch it several times a day on UHF, VHF and Cable.

Right: Ralph: 'One of these days, Alice, *one of these days*— Pow! Right in the kisser.' But at the show's end, he would say, 'Alice—you're the greatest.'

Right: Shirley Feeney (left, played by Cindy Williams) and Laverne De Fazio (Penny Marshall) flank Carmine Ragusa (Eddie Mekka); standing are Lenny Kolowski (Michael McKean, left) and Andrew 'Squiggy' Squiggman (David L Lander) in a scene from **Laverne and Shirley.** Lenny's last name was later changed to Kosnowski. The program began in 1976 and lasted until 1983. It was a spinoff of sorts from **Happy Days** (both girls had appeared briefly on that program) and was set in the same place and time as the parent show— Milwaukee of the 1950s. The two girls were spunky lower-class females with a lot of ambition, but they both worked on the assembly line at the bottle-cap division of the Shotz Brewery. Lenny and Squiggy both drove trucks at the plant, while Carmine, 'The Big Ragu,' was the amorous one of the group. During the 1977-78 season, it was the top rated show on television, despite its being called 'TV junk food.' Even its theme song, 'Making Our Dreams Come True,' written by Norman Gimbel and Charles Fox and sung by Cyndi Grecco, made the hit parade in 1976. A Saturday morning cartoon version ran from 1981-1983.

Left: Susan Saint James (left) plays Kate McArdle and Jane Curtin is Allie Lowell in **Kate and Allie,** an adult sitcom that premiered in 1984. It tells the story of two divorcees who share an apartment where they try to raise their kids. Kate is glamorous, contemporary and frivolous, while Allie is old-fashioned, industrious and proper. The chemistry between Saint James (a veteran of **The Name of the Game** from 1968 to 1971 and **McMillan and Wife** from 1971 to 1977) and Curtin (one of the original 'Not Ready for Prime Time' players from **Saturday Night Live**) is amazing. Their kids are Emma McArdle (Ari Meyers) and Chip and Jennie Lowell (Frederick Koehler and Allison Smith).

Right: The Odd Couple ran on ABC from 1970 to 1975 starring Tony Randall (left) as Felix Unger, the prim, fastidious photographer, and Jack Klugman as Oscar Madison, the gruff, sloppy sportswriter. Both were divorced and managed to co-exist in the same apartment in New York. The opening to the show always asked the same question, by way of a voice-over announcer 'Can two divorced men share an apartment without driving each other crazy? The answer was always a qualified yes, but each week they both seemed to be nearing insanity. The show was so well-done and popular that ABC tried to bring it back with **The New Odd Couple** in 1982. It starred Ron Glass and Demond Wilson.

Right: Bea Arthur as Dorothy (right) hugs her mother, Sophia (Estelle Getty) as her sister (Doris Belack) tries to persuade the mother that she should leave Dorothy and come to live with her in California in **The Golden Girls,** the hit sitcom about older people that premiered in 1985.

Below: Rhoda Morgenstern (Valerie Harper, left) lets her sister Brenda (Julie Kavner) in through the window in **Rhoda,** the spinoff from **The Mary Tyler Moore Show** that ran from 1974 to 1978. Rhoda had been Mary Richard's friend in Minneapolis, but left to come back home to New York, where she moved in with her sister and worked as a store window dresser. She met, married and then divorced Joe Gerard (David Groh) and went back to chubby Brenda, who had trouble getting dates. Two other stalwarts in the cast were Nancy Walker and Harold J Gould, who played the girls' parents, Ida and Martin Morgenstern. Lorenzo Music played the drunken Carlton the Doorman, although he was never seen. Only his voice was heard over the intercom from the lobby.

Above: Nicholas Colisanto played bartender Ernie 'Coach' Pantusso until his death, and Shelley Long is waitress Diane Chambers on **Cheers**, the story of life in a popular bar in Boston, which premiered in 1982. Much of the humor revolves around the barbs exchanged between Diane and her boss, ex-baseball pitcher Sam Malone (Ted Danson) and her co-worker, waitress Carla Tortelli (Rhea Perlman).

Right: Another spinoff from **The Mary Tyler Moore Show** was **Phyllis**, which ran from 1975 to 1977. Cloris Leachman (left) had the title role as the woman who had been Mary Richards' landlady. With her are daughter Bess (Lisa Gerritsen) and her friend Mark Valenti (Craig Wasson).

Above: Bea Arthur, as Maude, trying to shut up Rue McClanahan, as her best friend, Vivian Cavender Harmon. **Maude** was another spinoff from **All in the Family,** and ran from 1972 to 1978. Originally, Maude had appeared on that program as Edith Bunker's upper-middle-class, outspoken, liberal cousin. It was an unusual sitcom insofar as it explored some very serious subjects in a funny, yet serious, way—politics, face-lifts, abortion, menopause, bankruptcy, alcoholism. Also in the cast were Bill Macy as Maude's fourth husband, Walter Findlay, and Adrienne Barbeau as Carol, her daughter. Her first maid, Florida Evans was played by Esther Rolle. She and her TV husband, Henry (John Amos) left for the **Maude** spinoff, **Good Times,** where his name was changed to James.

Left: Serious dieting is a weighty issue for housemother Edna Garrett (Charlotte Rae, right), who is given a pep talk by teen-ager Blair Warner (Lisa Whelchel) in an episode of **The Facts of Life** called 'Dieting.' This program premiered on NBC as a spinoff of **Diff'rent Strokes** in 1979. On the previous show, Mrs Garrett had been the Drummond's housekeeper and she then moved to become a housemother at the prestigious Eastland School for Young Women. Later she became the dietician there. But she had differences with the administration and turned to running a gourmet food shop and catering business—, Edna's Edibles—and some of her former students moved in with her. In was on this program that movie star Molly Ringwald got her start.

SITUATION COMEDIES

Below: 'A horse is a horse, of course, of course.' Alan Young, as Wilbur Post, and Mr Ed, that talking Palomino. **Mr Ed** ran from 1961 to 1965 and was probably suggested by the old 'Francis the Talking Mule' films of years before. In this show of contrived nonsense, Post, a young architect, has just moved out of the city and inherits a horse that can talk (aided by the deep bass voice of Allan 'Rocky' Lane). The big problem was that Mr Ed would talk only to Wilbur, and everytime Wilbur mentioned that his horse could talk, everyone thought he was crazy. As strained and obviously based on a single joke as the show was, it won two Emmys. Ed was a typical sitcom character—cranky and ornery. Wilbur described him: 'Ed is a terrible slob who is good to his mother.'

Above: Dick York played Darrin Stephens and Elizabeth Montgomery was his wife, Samantha, who just happened to be a witch, in **Bewitched**, which ran on ABC from 1967 to 1972.

Below: Bob Denver (right) was castaway Gilligan and Alan Hale Jr was his marooned captain, Jonas 'The Skipper' Grumby, on **Gilligan's Island**, which ran on CBS from 1964 to 1967.

Opposite: Fred Gwynne was probably the only Harvard English major graduate and Shakespearean actor ever to play a Frankenstein's monster lookalike. He was Herman Munster on **The Munsters**, which appeared on CBS from 1964 to 1966. Yvonne DeCarlo played his wife Lily, who looked like a lady vampire. Son Eddie (Butch Patrick) looked like a juvenile werewolf and Grandpa (Al Lewis) looked like Dracula—Just your normal All-American family.

CRIME SHOWS

The crime fighter—whether a detective, a uniformed policeperson, a judge, a private eye, a secret agent, a T-man or a G-man, has been around on television for years. Perhaps it began with **Photocrime**, starring Chuck Webster as Inspector Hannibal Cobb, a program that lasted three months on ABC in 1949. But certainly the first enduring crime show was **Martin Kane, Private Eye**, which ran from 1949 to 1954 on NBC, and was carried on old kinescopes that appeared on stations away from New York a week or two late. Four men had the title role during its tenure—William Gargan, Lloyd Nolan, Lee Tracy and Mark Stevens. Later came **Rocky King, Inside Detective**, starring Roscoe Karns, lasting on Dumont from 1950 to 1954. Over the years, the crime shows became more believable, showing police work and law enforcement in general in a more realistic manner. **Dragnet** paved the way for that. Lawyers became more true-to-life and **Perry Mason** gave way to **The Defenders**. Crime shows won Emmys along the way as being best shows in a series—**Dragnet**, (three straight years), **The Defenders** (three straight years), **The Fugitive, Mission:Impossible** (two straight years), **Columbo, Police Story, The Rockford Files** and **Hill Street Blues** (four straight times). The crime show is with us to stay.

Left: Sergeant Joe Friday (played by Jack Webb)—everyone's favorite cop.

Dragnet was probably the most successful police series in television history, lasting on NBC from 1952 to 1959, and was revived from 1967 to 1970. Webb created the concept of the realistic, documentary-style show, directed the series, and played the lead. Based on files from the Los Angeles Police Department, the program gave us such catch-phrases as 'My name's Friday—I'm a cop,' 'Just the facts, Ma'am' and 'Book him on a 358.'

Opposite bottom: Harry Morgan (left) played in the 1967-1970 revival of **Dragnet**. Previous partners had been Barton Yarborough as Sergeant Ben Romero, Barney Phillips as Sergeant Ed Jacobs, Herb Ellis as Officer Frank Smith and Ben Alexander, who was Ben Smith from 1953 to 1959.

Above: Robert Stack (standing left) played Treasury Agent Elliott Ness in **The Untouchables** from 1959 to 1963. Seated at the end of the table is guest star Keenan Wynn. The show was a violent one featuring the chatter of machine-gun fire and the squeal of tires on the Chicago streets. The weekly bloodbath at times would feature two or three wild shootouts in a single hour. As **TV Guide** observed, 'In practically every episode a gang leader winds up stitched to a brick wall and full of bullets, or face down in a parking lot (and full of bullets), or hung up in an icebox, or run down in the street by a mug at the wheel of a big black Hudson touring car.' The program was based on the experiences of the real Elliott Ness and his T-men, in the twenties.

Above: The stars of **77 Sunset Strip**, which ran on ABC from 1958 to 1964, were private investigators Stuart Bailey (Efrem Zimbalist Jr, left), Gerald Lloyd 'Kookie' Kookson III (Edd Byrnes, center) and Jeff Spencer (Roger Smith). Kookie had started as a parking lot attendant and was taken into the firm.

Left: Michael Douglas (left) played Inspector Steve Keller and Karl Malden was Detective Lieutenant Mike Stone of the San Francisco Police Department in **The Streets of San Francisco**, which appeared on ABC from 1972 to 1977,

Top left: Dick Powell played wealthy detective Amos Burke in the 'Who Killed Julie Greer?' episode of **The Dick Powell Show** in 1962. The following year Gene Barry took on the same role in the series **Burke's Law.**

Opposite: Raymond Burr played the title role in **Perry Mason** from 1957 to 1966, with Barbara Hale playing his faithful secretary, Della Street.

Above: Kent McCord (left) as Officer Jim Reed, and Martin Milner, as Officer Pete Malloy, confront an elderly miscreant (Elizabeth Kerr) in **Adam 12**. A Jack Webb (meaning realistic) production on NBC from 1968 to 1975, it concerned the day-to-day grind of two patrol car policemen (Adam 12 was the number of their cruiser).

Top: Julie Barnes (Peggy Lipton), Linc Hayes (Clarence Williams III) and Pete Cochran (Michael Cole) in **Mod Squad** (1968-73, ABC)—three hippie undercover cops.
Opposite: Efrem Zimbalist Jr (left) played Inspector Lewis Erskine in **The FBI**, from 1965 to 1974 on ABC. It was a favorite of FBI director J Edgar Hoover.

Following spread: Stacey Keach plays Mike Hammer, a private investigator, on **Mickey Spillane's Mike Hammer**, which ran during 1984 and was revived in 1986. The hiatus was caused by Keach's imprisonment in England on a narcotics conviction. A thirty-minute version of the show had previously starred Darren McGavin from 1957 to 1959.

Right: Sharon Gless (left), as Detective Chris Cagney, and Tyne Daly (center), as Detective Mary Beth Lacey, confront guest star Elizabeth Ashley on **Cagney and Lacey**, which premiered on CBS in 1982.

Opposite top: Larry Wilcox (left) was Officer Jon Baker and Erik Estrada was Officer Frank 'Ponch' Poncherello in **CHIPS** (an acronym for California Highway Patrol), which ran on NBC from 1977 to 1983.

Opposite bottom: Jack Lord (left) and James McArthur of **Hawaii Five-O**, members of the Hawaiian State Police. The program ran for an astonishing 12 years—1968 to 1980.

Below: Charlie's Angels—left to right: Kate Jackson, as Sabrina Duncan, Farrah Fawcett-Majors as Jill Munroe, Cheryl Ladd as her sister Kris and Jaclyn Smith as Kelly Garrett, with David Doyle (right) as John Bosley. The show ran on ABC (1976 - 1980).

Right: Daniel Hugh Kelly (left) plays racing driver and two-time loser Mark 'Skid' McCormick and Brian Keith is the athletic retired Judge Milton G Hardcastle in **Hardcastle and McCormick**, which premiered on ABC in 1983. Together they track down the presumed criminals who have beaten the rap in Hardcastle's courtroom.

Opposite: Detective Mick Belker (Bruce Weitz, left) and Officer Andy Renko (Charles Haid) are stunned by a police slaying as a paramedic (Mello Alexandria) tends to the victim on the award-winning **Hill Street Blues**, which premiered on NBC in 1981.

Below: Daniel J Travanti (right) is Frank Furillo, the precinct captain on **Hill Street Blues**, Rene Enriquez plays Lieutenant Ray Calletano, one of his right-hand men on the police program.

Above: Remington Steele (played by Pierce Brosnan) warns his secretary Mildred Krebs (Doris Roberts) about hidden dangers on **Remington Steele**, the private eye program that started on NBC in 1982. Steele's love interest on the program is provided by Stephanie Zimbalist as his partner Laura Holt.

Above: A scene from **T J Hooker**. William Shatner, who played Sergeant Hooker of the 'LCPD,' is at center. Supposedly he had been a detective, but gave up his gold shield and mufti to become an officer on street patrol because that was where the action was. The program began on ABC in 1982, and Hooker found himself assigned to the police academy, where his traditional values were inculcated into his trainees. In 1983, however, the show featured one of his former probationers, Officer Stacy Sheridan (Heather Locklear) and her partner, Officer Jim Corrigan (James Darren) and their adventures, as well as Hooker's exploits. The show uses special guest stars, such as the Beach Boys and Jerry Lee Lewis. In one episode, Shatner had a reunion with his old friend from **Star Trek**—Leonard Nimoy—who played a man seeking revenge for the rape of his daughter.
Right: Riptide, starring Thom Bray, Joe Penny and Perry King, premiered in 1984.

Opposite: Angela Lansbury plays mystery writer Jessica Beatrice Fletcher on **Murder, She Wrote**, the program that has been on CBS since 1984. She lives in the tiny little town of Cabot Cove in Maine, and it wasn't until late in life that she became a celebrated author. Since her first best seller, she has traveled all over, and every week seems to be somewhere new and confronted by a new murder mystery. Of course she offers to help the police and ends up solving the crime and nailing the murderer. The show has two things going for it. First, it was the one that broke the barrier of youth worship by having a middle-aged person as a very capable and aware protagonist. Second, it eschews the usual blood and gore of the detective programs and offers the audience periodic clues.

Right: Occasionally **Lou Grant** (played by Edward Asner) delved into the subject of crime. Essentially this was a newspaper show that was a spinoff of **The Mary Tyler Moore Show**. Mary Richards' old boss, Lou, became the city editor of the **Los Angeles Tribune** a crusading newspaper. The program ran from 1977 to 1982, and in those brief five years, the program won 11 Emmys. Others in the cast included Robert Walden and Linda Kelsey as the reporters Joe Rossi and Billie Newman, Darryl Anderson as the photographer Dennis 'Animal' Price, Mason Adams as the managing editor Charlie Hume and Nancy Marchand, who played publisher Margaret Pynchon.

Opposite: Peter Falk, left, as Lieutenant **Columbo**, the seemingly incompetent bumbling detective in the wrinkled dirty raincoat. The series ran from 1971 to 1977 on NBC.

Below: Police lieutenant Frank Monahan (Garry Walberg, left) pleads with Dr Quincy, the coroner (Jack Klugman), not to interfere on **Quincy, ME**, which ran from 1976 to 1983

Left: Tom Selleck plays private detective Tom Magnum on **Magnum**, and Magnum should live the life of Riley. He lives free in Hawaii on the estate of a wealthy man, who is never seen on the show, in exchange for helping with the security arrangements for guarding the property. From his rambling beachfront lodge he charges out from time to time to fight crime—and earn a nice living. There also seems to be plenty of time for romance or for driving his $50,000 Ferrari. When he is on a case, this Naval Intelligence Vietnam veteran uses the services of two old buddies. There is Theodore 'T C' Calvin (Roger E Mosley), a former helicopter pilot, and Orville 'Rick' Wright (Larry Manetti). About the only real problems that Magnum has are caused by the stuffy, fussy British manservant, Jonathan Quayle Higgins III, played by John Hillerman (who was born in Dennison, Texas), who runs the estate in his master's absence. The show premiered in 1980.

Below and Opposite: Detective James 'Sonny' Crockett (played by Don Johnson, left in both pictures) and Detective Ricardo Tubbs (Philip Michael Thomas) are both vice cops in **Miami Vice**, which premiered in 1984 on NBC. Crockett is a rough-edged detective who lives aboard a sailboat, which he has cynically christened *St Vitus' Dance*, and guarded by Crockett's pet alligator, Elvis. Tubbs is a new arrival on the Miami scene. He is a former street cop from New York who had come south to find the murderer of his brother, and stayed on to be a Miami detective. These two make up an 'Odd Couple' team, but turn out to be quite effective as they chase vice criminals both on Miami's Gold Coast and the city's seedier sections. The show is different not only for the up-to-date costuming of the detectives, but also because of its heavy use of rock background music and music video effects. Shot in Miami, the show also features the city's Art-Deco district.

Above: Detective Dave Starsky (Paul Michael Glaser, left) and Detective Ken 'Hutch' Hutchinson (David Soul) on another case in **Starsky and Hutch**, the detective show that ran from 1975 to 1979 on ABC. In what seemed to be Los Angeles, they went to the toughest areas to seek out their prey—pimps, muggers, dope pushers and general hoodlums. Starsky was street-wise and drove a bright red 1974 Ford Torino hot-rod. Hutch was the better-educated, soft-spoken one.

Right: Moonlighting premiered in 1985 on ABC and soon became regarded as the classiest private detective show on television. The chemistry between Cybill Shepherd and Bruce Willis, as a team of private eyes, is electric, and the dialogue is fast-paced and sometimes sardonic. The direction and photography can be most interesting, too. Shepherd and Willis play Maddie Hayes and David Addison who gradually realize that they are mutually attracted. They advance for their first kiss, and the scene is blacked out.

Above: Mannix was played by Mike Connors (the former Touch Connors), and he was a Los Angeles-based private detective. It was one of the most violent of the detective shows, and also one of the most long-lived, running from 1967 to 1975 on CBS. Mannix was a rebel. He worked for a sophisticated detective firm called Interect—a company that used computers and other sophisticated detection aids. Still, Mannix preferred to work with his own intuition, his revolver and his fists. That, lasted one season, and the next year, he had set himself up in his own small office. Every episode seemed to contain a wild brawl. It also seemed that there was an extremely high body count, even during the first few minutes of each show. Aiding Connors in all this was Gail Fisher (as his secretary, and girl-Friday, Peggy Fair).

Above: Steve Forrest was Lieutenant Dan 'Hondo' Harrelson on **S.W.A.T.** (the acronym for Special Weapons and Tactics). This was a program about police squads who use violent army-style ware, and it ran on ABC from 1975 to 1976.
Left: Detective Tony Baretta (Robert Blake) with Fred, his pet cockatoo, in **Baretta**, an ABC detective show that from 1975 to 1978. Baretta, a street-wise bachelor cop, was pretty unconventional, living in a run-down hotel, usually seen wearing a T-shirt and jeans. Not only that, he was a master of disguise, and was able to infiltrate motorcycle gangs and other mobs. And he worked alone. What really made the show different was the comic relief.

SCIENCE-FICTION SHOWS

Captain Video and His Video Rangers was surely the first science-fiction program on television. It was first seen on the Dumont Network in 1949 and lasted until 1955. Richard Coogan was the original 'Guardian of the Safety of the World,' from 1949 to 1950, then the role was taken over by Al Hodge. 'The cereals made by Post . . .take you to the secret mountain retreat of. . .**Captain Video! Master of Space! Hero of Science! Captain of the Video Rangers!** Operating from his secret mountain headquarters on the planet Earth, Captain Video rallies men of good will and leads them against the forces of evil everywhere! As he rockets from planet to planet, let us follow the champion of justice, truth and freedom through the universe! Stand by for. . .**Captain Video. . .and his Video Rangers!**' Clad in a costume of military uniform, laced combat boots and headgear made to look like a football helmet with goggles, Captain Video would deal with his space ship, his enemies and Tobor (robot spelled backwards)—the unstoppable machine that worked for the good of mankind. And all this on a prop budget of $25 per week. The next year there was **Tom Corbett, Space Cadet,** starring Frankie Thomas in the title role, which lasted for two years on ABC. In 1951 came **Space Patrol,** also an ABC show, which ran from 1951 to 1952 starring Ed Kemmer. and spent a magnificent $2500 on every episode. Then there was CBS's **Rod Brown of the Rocket Rangers** starring a very young Cliff Robertson; **Commando Cody, Rocky Jones, Space Rangers** and **Captain Z-RO.** 'Smokin' rockets, Commander,' it was only 1955, and television was hardly out of its diapers. Over the years we have had time travelers **(Time Tunnel, Voyagers),** travelers beneath the surface of the Earth **(Voyage to the Bottom of the Sea),** travelers in outer space **(Lost in Space),** space warriors **(Star Trek, Battlestar Galactica),** and protagonists of other species **(Planet of the Apes, The Outer Limits)** and just plain strange situations **(The Twilight Zone, Thriller).** The world of science fiction is just too much fun to perform and too much fun to watch for television to abandon it.

Above: Battlestar Galactica was television's answer to the film **Star Wars** (1977), and the producers of the movie sued ABC about that. Actually, the special effects of both were created by the same man, John Dykstra. The show cost $1 million per hour to produce, yet it ran for just the 1979 season. Revived as **Galactica 1980,** it ran for eight months and died again. Here Lorne Greene, as Commander Adama, joins two members of his crew in wedlock.
Right: Marta Kristen, as Judy Robinson, and Mark Goddard, as Major Donald West, in **Lost in Space.** The five 'Space Family Robinsons,' along with West, were on a five-year space exploration, but the ship's control system was sabotaged, and they wandered from planet to planet from 1965 to 1968 on CBS
Opposite: The other members of the **Lost in Space** cast were Jonathan Harris, as Dr Zachary Smith, the man who had done the sabotage and then was trapped on the ship, and a friendly, logical, ambulatory robot.

Opposite: The grandaddy of all science-fiction shows on television was **Captain Video and His Video Rangers**. Through most of its run from 1949 to 1953 it was a five-times-a-week, half-hour show—quite a strain on the cast. Al Hodge (left) played Captain Video and Don Hastings was the Ranger. Among the villains that the captain fought over the years were Nargola, Mook the Moon Man, Kul of Eos, Heng Foo Seeng, Dr Clysmok and Dahoumi. But the worst of all was Dr Pauli (Hal Conklin), the head of the Astroidal Society. Kids loved the show and bought Captain Video records, toy rocket sets, comic books, dolls, stationery, trading cards, bedspreads, wallets, clothes and dishes.

Above: Hard on the heels of Captain Video was **Rocky Jones, Space Ranger** a sci-fi kid's show that surfaced in the mid 1950s. It starred Richard Crane (left, helping to release the beautiful captive) in the title role, and was the first space show made exclusively for television entirely on film. Jimmy Lydon is at right.
Left: Another popular science fiction children's program was the Saturday morning feature **Stingray**. This one used puppets, and it was a well-produced show, although pretty simplistic. The heroes were the Wasps—referring to the insect, not to any social group in American society. Kids liked it, although they were to appreciate Jim Henson's Muppets more especially in the 'Pigs in Space' segments.

Above: It's hard to believe, considering all the hullabaloo about the program, that **Star Trek** was not a particularly popular program the first time around. It lasted only three years on NBC, from 1966 to 1969, and in its best year was ranked a poor 52nd in the series ratings—just behind **Iron Horse** and **Mr Terrific**. Then came the reruns and the cult fans, called 'Trekkies' and the subsequent movies. In this scene, arch villain Khan (second from left), played by Ricardo Montalban, is banished to a barren planet by Captain Kirk in an episode called 'Space Seed,' aired in 1967. The episode was later expanded into the plot for the film **Star Trek II: The Wrath of Khan**, with Montalban back in the saddle.
Right: William Shatner prepared to defend himself on **Star Trek**. Shatner played Captain James T Kirk (later promoted to admiral in the films as a deference to his age), the comander of the starship USS *Enterprise*, a cruiser-sized spacecraft, whose mission included reconnaissance of unexplored worlds and transporting supplies to Earth colonies in space. The crew also had problems in skirmishes with two alien races, the Klingons and the Romulans. The stories were well written and often reflected on current social issues.
Opposite: The three main characters from **Star Trek** Captain Kirk, (Shatner), Dr Leonard 'Bones' McCoy (DeForest Kelley) and Mr Spock (Leonard Nimoy). McCoy was a fine surgeon and diagnostician with a sarcastic sense of humor. Spock was a half-breed Vulcan whose father had been a Vulcan ambassador and whose mother was an Earthling. His problem was that he had a totally logical mind, but this contrasted nicely with Kirk's impetuosity.

Above: Roddy McDowall recreated his film role as Galen, the intelligent ape in **Planet of the Apes**, which ran a mere four months on CBS in 1974. Later, NBC aired an animated version called **Beyond the Planet of the Apes**, which was seen Saturday mornings from 1975 to 1976.

Right: Gil Gerard was Captain William 'Buck' Rogers, and Erin Gray was his girl friend Wilma Deering on **Buck Rogers in the 25th Centuy**, which ran from 1979 to 1980 on NBC and was resurrected from January to April 1981. There had been an ABC version, of the old comic strip, called **Buck Rogers**, in 1950 and 1951, but this updated show was far more elaborate. It had fancy special effects and was done tongue-in-cheek. Rogers had been frozen in suspended animation for 500 years and was thawed out to defend Earth against the Draconians.

Above right: Diana (Jane Bader, right) one of the evil leaders of the aliens from outer space, is furious when she realizes she has killed one of her own people rather than the enemy in **V: The Final Battle**, an NBC mini-series of 1984.

Opposite: The cast of **Logan's Run** which ran on CBS in 1977-78. included Gregory Harrison, Heather Menzies, Donald Moffat and Randy Powell.

ADVENTURE SHOWS

The adventure show genre is hard to define, since it almost defies catagorization. Some of them are humorous—some are serious. Some of them are fanciful, some are down-to earth and realistic. But they all involve great exploits that cannot be classified as crime shows or science-fiction shows or drama shows. Some of them involve super-heroes **(The Six Million Dollar Man)**. Some of them involve average people doing their dangerous jobs **(Call to Glory, Airwolf, The Fall Guy)**. Many of them involved teams. Often these teams consist of just two people. **(The Man from U.N.C.L.E, Batman, The Green Hornet, The Wild, Wild West)**. Then there were many that involve much larger teams **(Mission: Impossible, The A-Team)**. But most of them have been popular programs that offered escapism to the viewing audience. The adventure show is not one of the oldest of the various categories of television entertainment. These shows had to wait until the mechanics of special effects had been developed in order to serve them. Indeed, they had to wait until enough money was spent in order to create these special effects. Perhaps the first show of this type was **Lights Out,** which ran on NBC from 1949 to 1952. It was a suspense anthology, broadcast live, and featured stories of mystery, suspense and the supernatural. At the beginning of each episode, viewers could see only a close shot of a pair of eyes, then a bloody hand reaching to turn out the lights, followed by an eerie laugh and the words, 'Lights out, everybody. . .' At first the show used little-known actors but as it became more popular, such guest stars as Boris Karloff, Burgess Meredith, Basil Rathbone and Raymond Massey would show up.

Right: James Phelps (Peter Graves, center) was the leader of the **Mission: Impossible** teams, and Barney Collier (Greg Morris, right) was the team's electronics expert. Each episode would begin with Phelps receiving a tape-recorded message telling him the details of the job he was being asked to take on, whether it be to disrupt the activities of a foreign power or organized crime in the United States. The plans executed by the Impossible Missions Force were always incredibly complex. The show ran on CBS from 1966 to 1973.

Left: Ilya Kuryakin (David McCallum, left) and Napoleon Solo (Robert Vaughn) were the superagents in **The Man From U.N.C.L.E.** a takeoff of the James Bond movies. Working for **U**nited **N**etwork **C**ommand for **L**aw and **E**nforcement, they fought the international crime syndicate THRUSH. The show ran on NBC from 1964 to 1968.

Below: Sergeant Bosco 'B A' Baracus (Mr T, left) is the strong man and mechanical expert, and Captain H M 'Howling Mad' Murdoch (Dwight Schultz) is the insane pilot on **The A-Team**, the series featuring a soldier of fortune organization that fights injustice wherever it is found. For some reason, they seldom take a fee, although the

complicated plots require the expenditure of a vast amount of money. Despite jeeps spinning through the air and buildings leveled in fiery explosions, no one—not even the bad guys—ever gets hurt. But, as B A would say, 'You better watch out, sucker.' The program premiered on NBC in 1983, replacing **Father Murphy**.

Above: Batman was the pop show hit of 1966 through 1968, and was so popular that it ran twice a week. Here are Burt Ward (left) as Robin, the Boy Wonder, and Adam West as Batman, standing beside the Batmobile—that marvelously equipped jet car. Batman was 'The Caped Crusader' and Robin was 'The Boy Wonder.' Together, they were 'The Dynamic Duo,' and fought crime whenever their services were required by Police Commissioner Gordon (played by Neil Hamilton). In real life, they were Bruce Wayne, a rich orphan, and his young ward, another orphan, Dick Grayson. It was the ultimate 'camp' show of the 1960s. The fight scenes were punctuated with animated cartoon 'Pows,' 'Bops,' Bangs' and 'Thuds' that flashed on the screen whenever a blow was struck. The pair maintained an underground 'Batlab' containing all manner of crime-fighting equipment—all carefully labeled, of course, and in their den was a red batphone,' with direct access to the Commissioner's office. The only one who knew their real identities was Wayne's faithful family butler Alfred Pennyworth (Alan Napier), who had raised him when his parents were murdered.

Left: Show business personalities would kill to be the guest villain on **Batman**—and Joan Collins was no exception. Along the way, such luminaries as Burgess Meredith (as the Penguin), Cesar Romero (The Joker), Vincent Price (Egghead), Frank Gorshin (The Riddler), John Astin (also The Riddler), Victor Buono (King Tut), and, at various times, Julie Newmar, Lee Ann Meriweather and Eartha Kitt (as The Catwoman). The program ran out of steam quickly, even though Commissioner Gordon's daughter Barbara (Yvonne Craig) was brought in as Batgirl.

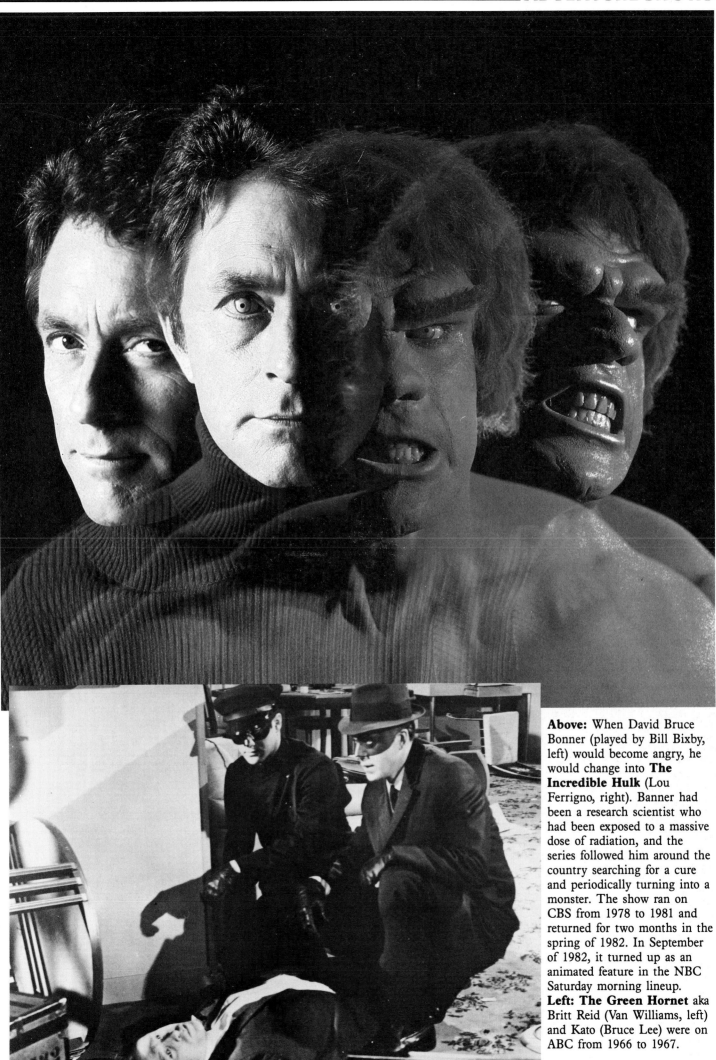

Above: When David Bruce Bonner (played by Bill Bixby, left) would become angry, he would change into **The Incredible Hulk** (Lou Ferrigno, right). Banner had been a research scientist who had been exposed to a massive dose of radiation, and the series followed him around the country searching for a cure and periodically turning into a monster. The show ran on CBS from 1978 to 1981 and returned for two months in the spring of 1982. In September of 1982, it turned up as an animated feature in the NBC Saturday morning lineup.
Left: The Green Hornet aka Britt Reid (Van Williams, left) and Kato (Bruce Lee) were on ABC from 1966 to 1967.

89

Above: Jan-Michael Vincent played the part of Stringfellow Hawke on the foreign intrigue series **Airwolf** which was also the name of his helicopter. The show premiered on CBS in 1984 Hawke was the pilot recruited by the US Government agency known as 'The Firm' to retrieve this high-tech machine (it was faster than a jet and had a lot of firepower and a range of halfway around the world) when it was stolen. Hawke got it back, but wouldn't return it to the government until the US found his brother, a MIA in Vietnam. In the meantime, Hawke agreed to go on missions for The Firm in this awesome copter.

Left: Call to Glory, the short-lived program that premiered on ABC in 1984, was set in the early 1960s during the cold war, and starred Craig T Nelson as Colonel Raynor Sarnac of the US Air Force. He was in command of a group of jet pilots who got involved in the crises of the times—such as the Cuban Missile Crisis and the beginning involvement in Vietnam. The program also focused on his problems with his home life.

Left: Chris George (left) played Sargeant Sam Troy, the leader of the pack, and Gary Raymond was Sergeant Jack Moffitt on **The Rat Patrol**, which ran on ABC from 1966 to 1968. There were four men in the patrol. In addition to Troy, the head rat, and Moffitt, the British demolitions expert (he was quite necessary, since there were explosions going off all the time on this program), there were Private Mark Hitchcock (Lawrence Casy), who was trying to live down his sissy reputation, and Private Tully Pettigrew (Justin Tarr), the charming con man. Their usual enemy was Hauptmann Hans Dietrich (Hans Gudegast), the commanding officer of a German armored unit, in General Erwin Rommel's elite Afrika Korps during the North African desert campaign in World War II.

Right: Lee Majors (formerly **The Six Million Dollar Man**) switched to playing the stuntman Colt Seavers in **The Fall Guy,** which premiered on ABC in 1981. Seavers worked his stunts on the Hollywood back lots and also picked up some spare change by hiring himself out to track down and capture bail jumpers. Assisting him were his cousin Howie Munson (Douglas Barr) and stuntwoman Jody Bank (Heather Thomas). The assignments for this intrepid trio were handed out by sexy bail bondswomen—Jo Ann Pflug played Samantha, 'Big Jack' Jack during the first year of the series, and Markie Post was Terri Shannon (whose name was later changed to Terri Michaels) the next year. Spectacular stunt work was the hallmark of this action series, which was Majors' fifth successful prime-time offering. In addition to **The Six Million Dollar Man** (1974-1978, ABC), Majors appeared in **The Big Valley** (1965-1969 ABC), **The Virginian** (late in the series—1970-1971, NBC) and **Owen Marshall, Counselor at Law** (1971-1974, ABC)

Right: Darren McGavin is ready to fend off a vampire in an episode of **Kolchak: The Night Stalker**, which appeared from 1974 through 1975 on ABC. McGavin played Carl Kolchak, a crime reporter for Chicago's Independent News Service, an investigative type who kept running into vampires, werewolves, zombies and other phenomena. For example, the time that he was sent to investigate a crooked politician, he found that the man had sold his soul to the Devil; mummies came alive at museum openings. Kolchak's big problem in this tongue-in-cheek mystery show was in convincing his editor, Tony Vincenzo (played by Simon Oakland), that what he was reporting was true. McGavin's career on television has been a long and distinguished one. He started out in the early days, playing Casey, the **Crime Photographer**, on CBS in 1951. From 1957 to 1959, he was Mike on the original **Mickey Spillane's Mike Hammer**, a syndicated show. From 1959 to 1961, he played the captain of a stern-wheeler, in **Riverboat** on NBC. In 1968 and 1969 he was David Ross, a private eye, on NBC's **The Outsider**. In 1983 he was another private eye, Nick Small, on CBS's **Small & Frye**.

Left: Robert Conrad was James T West on CBS's **The Wild Wild West** from 1965 to 1969, and then again in the summer of 1970. West was the James Bond of the nineteenth century Western. He was an undercover agent for President Grant, who would send him and his partner Artemus Gordon (Ross Martin) to expose, or at least undermine, various radical, revolutionary or criminal groups who wanted to take over various parts of the United States. The pair had a private railroad car that served as their headquarters and in which they developed Bond-like weapons and devices to use in their derring-do. One of the many villains was a dwarf who kept showing up, much as the Cat-Woman kept showing up in **Batman**—Dr Miguelito Loveless, played by Michael Dunne, a brilliant antagonist who wanted to own the world.

Above: The Twilight Zone was a brilliant anthology of weird half-hour dramas, hosted by Rod Serling, who wrote many of the scripts. It ran on CBS from 1959 to 1963, and then in the 1963-64 season expanded to one hour. In this episode, Agnes Moorehead is a farm wife confronted by a tiny visitor from outer space.
Left: John Schneider (Bo Duke), Catherine Bach (Daisy Duke) and Tom Wopat (Luke Duke) lie on their souped up Dodge Charger, 'General Lee' in **The Dukes of Hazzard**, a rural adventure show that premiered on CBS in 1979. When Wopat and Schneider walked out in 1982, they were replaced by Byron Cherry and Christopher Mayer.

DRAMA

Almost from the very beginning, drama has been part of the life-blood of television. In 1947, when it was broacasting a mere eight and one-half hours of network programs per week, NBC gave over one hour of that time to the **Kraft Television Theatre**, a distinguished series that was to last until 1958. By the end of its run, this Wednesday night institution had presented 650 plays—drama and comedy, original and adaptation. The program did Shakespeare and Ibsen, and Tennessee Williams, Agatha Christie and Rod Serling. In 1948 **Studio One** appeared on CBS and was destined to run until 1958. Its first play was an adaptation of the mystery play **The Storm**, with Margaret Sullavan. **Studio One** put on some 500 plays during its tenure. NBC premiered the **Philco TV Playhouse** which continued until 1955, in that same year of 1948, and the network also presented the **Chevrolet Tele-Theatre** from 1948 to 1950. So from nothing in 1946, drama went from one hour per week in 1947 to two and one-half hours per week in 1948. Just five years later, these shows (and by then there were two **Kraft Television Theaters** on the air, one hour on NBC and one hour on ABC) were joined by **Robert Montgomery Presents, The US Steel Hour, The Motorola Video Theatre, The Philip Morris Playhouse, The Four Star Playhouse, Ford Theatre, Showcase Theater, The Pepsi-Cola Playhouse, The Schlitz Playhouse of Stars** and **The Medallion Theater**. Not all of them were great, but it was quite a weekly choice. We will never see that kind of lineup again, but in those days there were no dramatic specials and mini-series.

Above: Katharine Hepburn as the idealistic schoolmistress who finds one boy with the spark of creativity in a Welsh mining village, in the 1979 television adaptation of Emlyn Williams' play **The Corn Is Green**—a made-for-television movie.

Left: Studio One launched its season in 1954 with one of the finest television dramas in history, Reginald Rose's taut jury-room drama **Twelve Angry Men**. Left to right, the members of the jury: Norman Feld, John Beal, Lee Philips (seated), Franchot Tone, Bart Burns, Robert Cummings, Paul Hartman, Walter Abel (standing), Edward Arnold, Joseph Sweeny, George Voskovec and Will West. The play won three Emmys: writing (Reginald Rose), direction (Frank Schaffner) and acting (Robert Cummings). It was later made into a movie starring Henry Fonda and Lee J Cobb.

Below: Husband and wife team Natalie Wood and Robert Wagner starred with Laurence Olivier (center, playing 'Big Daddy'), in the made-for-television film **Cat on a Hot Tin Roof**, adapted from Tennessee Williams' play. Wood played the wife of a former football hero (Wagner), who is dominated by alcohol, homosexuality and his father (Olivier). It was the story of a warped family on a Mississippi Delta plantation, and the film was a result of an international agreement, among NBC, Granada Television of Great Britain and Laurence Olivier himself, and it was a blockbuster.

Left: Sophia Loren starred in a dual role in a made-for-television movie in 1980—**Sophia Loren—Her Own Story**. In the early part of the film (as shown here) she played her own mother. Later in the movie she played herself.

Left: Jack Hawkins played his last role as Justice Gilray, the presiding judge in the final courtroom scenes of one of the longest films ever made for television, **QB VII**, based on Leon Uris' best-selling novel. Shown in 1974, the film was a mini-series, running nearly six hours, and telling the story of a knighted Polish expatriate, Dr. Adam Kelno (Anthony Hopkins), living in England, and the libel suit he initiated against an American writer, Abe Cady (Ben Gazarra), for accusing him in his book of performing criminal medical practices in a concentration camp during World War II. Kelno's life was covered in fascinating flashbacks that were shot in Israel, England, Belgium and the United States. The final scenes in the courtroom where accuser becomes the accused, were shattering.

Opposite top: John Amos, as the older Kunta Kinte, and Madge Sinclair as his wife, Bell, bid a heart-wrenching goodbye to their daughter, Kizzy (Leslie Uggams) in **Roots** the phenomenally popular mini-series of 1977. based on Alex Haley's monumental book, the ABC series was the most-watched dramatic show in American television history. It was shown for eight straight nights, and the final installment was watched by approximately 100 million people—almost half of the population of the country. The story was the story of the author's own roots, beginning in Gambia in 1750, with the birth of Kunta Kinte, who was captured by slavers and shipped to America. It ended with Tom, his great-grandson, finding freedom on his farm in 1882. It was so popular that the whole series was repeated the following year and a sequel of seven episodes was made, bringing the story up to the present.

Left: Barry Bostwick starred in the title role of **George Washington**, a mini-series about the early life of the first president, in 1984 on CBS.

Opposite bottom: A scene from ABC's **The Day After**. showing the results of the final atomic holocaust.

Above: Richard Chamberlain and Rachel Ward starred in **The Thorn Birds**, a 1983 mini-series based on Colleen McCullough's novel about a handsome Australian parish priest, Father Ralph de Bricassart (Chamberlain), and his relationship with young Meggie. Also in the cast of 'Australia's **Gone With the Wind**' was Barbara Stanwyck, as the 75-year-old wealthy and spiteful matriarch of 'Drogheda,' one of the most prosperous sheep stations in Australia, who also lusts after Father Ralph. Indeed, Stanwyck stole the entire first three hours of this ten-hour program.

Left: Peter O'Toole, as the weary, embattled General Cornelius Flavius Silva in **Masada**, the 1980, seven and a half hour mini-series about the Judean desert war which ended in 70 AD, between the Jews and the Roman Army. Somehow it avoided all the pitfalls of the typical 'Biblical drama,' and was a magnificent entertainment, with the never-better O'Toole dominating.

Opposite: Richard Chamberlain, the king of the television mini-series, as the Englishman Blackthorne, and Yoko Shimada, as his interpreter, being led on their horses in the 1980 eight and a half hour mini-series, **Shogun**. Based on James Clavell's novel about feudal Japan, it included raging storms, shipwrecks, head-slicing Samurai, prisons, beautiful ladies, conniving priests and the ways of the ruling class, including ritual suicide and its traditions. The scenery, the action and the authenticity were magnificent. Also in the outstanding cast was the renowned Toshiro Mifune.

Above: A passle from **The Waltons**—Tom Bower (Dr Curtiss Willard), Judy Norton-Taylor (Mary Ellen), Richard Thomas (John Boy), Kami Cotler (Elizabeth), Ellen Corby (Grandma Esther) and Will Geer (Grandpa Zeb).

Right: Richard Thomas, as John Boy Walton, and Ralph Waite, as his father, John, try to cheer up Erica Hunton on **The Waltons**, which ran on CBS from 1972 to 1981.

Opposite: Melissa Gilbert played Laura Ingalls and Michael Landon was her father, Charles Ingalls, on **Little House on the Prairie**, which ran on NBC from 1974 to 1983. Based on the autobiographical books by Laura Ingalls Wilder, the program's setting was the 1870s and told the story of a loving family on a homestead near the little town of Walnut Grove, Minnesota. The family consisted, in the beginning, of Charles and his wife, Caroline, and their three daughters, Mary, Laura and Carrie.

SOAPS

The serials—soap operas—have been strong for years. They began on radio in the early 1930s, switched to television in the 1950s, and are still as popular as ever. Probably their greatest fans are women, and there's a reason for that. The daytime soaps were important ego-builders for women long before anyone ever heard of Women's Liberation. Women on soaps have always been portrayed as doctors, judges, teachers, social workers, once, even a senator. On nighttime television, women are usually portrayed as having little effect on the social order, outside of their sexual role. On **Search for Tomorrow**, Kathy Phillips was an ambitious lawyer, Julie Franklin was a psychotherapist on **How to Survive a Marriage**; Althea Davis was one of the most important physicians on **The Doctors**. Sometimes soaps have been in the forefront of pointing out previously taboo subjects. Years ago, **Love of Life** had a character who made visits to a clinic for sexual dysfunction and discussed the delicate problem of male impotence; **The Young and the Restless** showed Chris Brooks, a young rape victim, bear witness against her attacker in court and then lose the case—unfortunately, this is what often happens in real life. Cancer, drug addiction, rape, venereal disease, the right to die, divorce, promiscuity, and many other subjects have been more forthrightly treated on the soaps than on prime

time television, and in a more honest way. In reality, television drama did not disappear—it went to daytime serials. A few years ago, Academy Award-winner Joanne Woodward was asked where she thought the best acting on television was, and she answered, 'Why, on the daytime serials. If I ever went back to television it would be on a soap.'

Top: Rosemary Prinz (left) was in at the beginning of **As the World Turns**. She played Penny Hughes on the premiere telecast on 2 April 1956. Konrad Matthaei was the criminal Roy McGuire, who let his wife Sandy be sent to prison for his own nefarious deeds. Sandy was paroled and married Penny's brother Bob.
Opposite: A tender moment on the beach in **All My Children**, which is probably the only light-hearted soap on the air, but is a home-and-family program.
Right: Peyton Place was probably the first prime time soap, running from 1964 to 1969 on ABC, seething with extramarital affairs, dark secrets and skulduggery.

Above: Search for Tomorrow premiered on CBS 3 September 1951 and still seems to be more concerned with character development than relevancy.

Left: There was a double wedding on **Days of Our Lives** (the NBC soap that premiered on 8 November 1965) on 14 February 1986. Pete Jannings (played by Michael Leon, top left) married Melissa Anderson (Lisa Trusel, seated left) and Mickey Horton (John Clarke) married Maggie Horton (Suzanne Rogers). Clarke had been with the program since its inception, and Mickey and Maggie Horton were having another go at marriage, since their first marriage to each other had ended in divorce three years before. The unifying character on the show is Dr Tom Horton (played by Macdonald Carey, one of the first real Hollywood stars to appear on a soap), who intones in a voice-over at the start of every program, 'Like sands through the hour-glass, so are the days of our lives.'

Left: Jonathan Frid played a vampire, Barnabas Collins on **Dark Shadows**, which premiered on ABC 27 June 1966. It was a weird show and featured every device ever used in horror-supernatural movies—live burials, living corpses, strange bedeviled young men, unknown ailments, nutty conjurers and witches. Frid was soon receiving more than a thousand fan letters a day—mostly from teenage girls. The camera work was not great, however, and often the overhead equipment would appear.

Above: Nick Nolte (left) played Tom Jordache and Peter Strauss was his brother Rudy in **Rich Man, Poor Man**, the soap opera-like mini-series that ran on ABC in 1976. Susan Blakely was Rudy's life-long love, Julie Prescott Abbott.
Below: The Edge of Night is television's only crime/mystery soap. It premiered on ABC 2 April 1956 and won an Emmy for best daytime drama in 1972. Here are Ann Flood (playing Nancy Pollock) and Forrest Compton (as Mike Karr, who eventually married Nancy).

Above: The gang from **Dallas**, the nighttime soap that began on CBS in 1978: Ray Krebbs (played by Steve Kanaly), Bobby Ewing (Patrick Duffy), Pamela Barnes Ewing (Victoria Principal), Eleanor Southworth 'Miss Ellie' Ewing (Barbara Bel Geddes), John Ross 'Jock' Ewing (Jim Davis), Lucy Ewing Cooper (Charlene Tilton), John Ross 'J.R.' Ewing Jr (Larry Hagman) and Sue Ellen Ewing (Linda Gray).

Right: One of **Dallas'** more succesful imitators was **Dynasty**. It premiered on ABC in 1981, telling the story of a group of people, all of whom were either filthy rich and disgusting or not-so-rich and disgusting. Here Blake Carrington (John Forsythe) remonstrates with his nemesis and former wife, Alexis Carrington Colby (Joan Collins).

Opposite: Joan Van Ark as Valene Ewing in **Knots Landing**, a spinoff of **Dallas**, which premiered on CBS in 1979.

Above: One of the strangest of the soaps was the late night syndicated show **Mary Hartman, Mary Hartman,** created by Norman Lear which premiered in 1976. It lasted for two years. The problems faced by this 'typical American housewife' of Fernwood, Ohio, were unbelievable. Here Mary (Louise Lasser) discusses his impotency with her husband, Tom (Greg Mullavey). She also had to cope with 'dirty yellow buildup' on the kitchen floor, her daughter Heather's being kidnapped by a mass murderer, her grandfather's penchant for exposing himself in public (he was known as 'The Fernwood Flasher'), the electrocution of an eight-year-old evangelist in the bathtub, and other crises.

Right: General Hospital, first appeared on ABC on 1 April 1963. An episode that probably every college student in the country watched (they used to gather in front of their television set dressed in white costumes and carrying little doctors' bags filled with cans of beer—just to watch **General Hospital**), was the wedding of Luke (Tony Geary) and Laura (Genie Francis), and the world held its breath. It was the ultimate reconciliation, since he had previously raped her. Laura had had a hard life. She was never sure who her parents were and she had spent time in a commune in Haverland, Canada, where a Charles Manson-type sexually abused the girls.

Above right: Greg Reardon (Simon McCorkindale) gathers evidence to help Angela Channing (Jane Wyman) save her estate, **Falcon Crest**. The show premiered as a nighttime soap in 1981 on CBS in the time slot following **Dallas**, and Jane Wyman proved to be the same type of autocratic, evil power broker in her wine country as Larry Hagman, as J R Ewing was in his oil fields on **Dallas**.

Right: The Guiding Light premiered on CBS in 1952, and the original stars were Charita Bauer (who played Bert Bauer) and Theo Goetz (who played her father-in-law, Papa Bauer).

WESTERNS

The cowboy show has always been a staple of television. True, their popularity comes and goes, but they always seem to reappear. In the second year of Dumont's network broadcasting, 1947, they were airing Western movies for an hour every Tuesday night. Ten years later the tube was awash with oaters. Sunday night gave us **Maverick** (ABC). On Monday there were **Restless Gun** and **Tales of Wells Fargo** (both NBC). Tuesday's lineup included **Cheyenne, Sugarfoot, The Life and Legend of Wyatt Earp** and **Broken Arrow** (all on ABC) plus **The Californians** (NBC). On Wednesday there were **Tombstone Territory** (ABC) and **Wagon Train** (NBC). Thursday gave us **Zorro** (ABC). On Friday there were **The Adventures of Rin Tin Tin, The Adventures of Jim Bowie** and **Colt .45** (all ABC) plus **Trackdown** (CBS). Finally, on Saturday we could watch **Have Gun, Will Travel** and **Gunsmoke** (both CBS). Seventeen in one week was a bit much, even for Western buffs. But television is rather lonesome now without them. All we can do is hope. The detective shows made a big comeback. Perhaps so will the horse operas. Where is Lorne Greene when we need him?

Above: The Lone Ranger (played by Clayton Moore) and his faithful Indian companion, Tonto (Jay Silverheels), were a media staple. The program had begun on a local Detroit radio station in 1933 and then moved to the new Mutual Broadcasting System. By 1934, the youth of American had learned that the theme song was Rossini's William Tell Overture—probably the only piece of classical music that most of them could identify. **The Lone Ranger** hit television on ABC in 1949 (with Moore and Silverheels). Moore stayed on until 1952, when John Hart took over. But Moore was back in 1954, and played the title role until the show had its last telecast in 1957.

Left: Richard Boone starred as Paladin in **Have Gun, Will Travel** on CBS from 1957 to 1963. He was a West Point-educated intellectual who, after the Civil War, went to San Francisco to be a 'gun for hire.' But he was an ethical troubleshooter—intimidating, but with a penchant for the finest clothes, epicurean meals and literate company, when he was not out on a job.

Opposite: Hoss (played by Dan Blocker, left) and Little Joe (Michael Landon)—two of the sons of Ben Cartwright (Lorne Greene, right) in **Bonanza,** the classic Western on NBC from 1959 to 1973.

Above: Some of the **Gunsmoke** gang: Dr Galen 'Doc' Adams (Milburn Stone); Sam, the bartender (Glenn Strange); Miss Kitty Russell (Amanda Blake); Marshal Matt Dillon (James Arness); Festus Haggen (Ken Curtis) and Newly O'Brien (Buck Taylor). The program had begun on radio in 1952, with William Conrad as the voice of Matt Dillon. When CBS decided they would put the program on television, they first apprached John Wayne to play Dillon. Wayne didn't want to commit himself to the rigors of a weekly television series, and suggested James Arness.

Above: Guy Williams played Don Diego de la Vega, aka **Zorro** on ABC from 1957 to 1959. It was a show produced by Walt Disney, and featured the swashbuckling hero in Spanish California in 1820. He returned from Spain to find that a ruthless army officer was tyrannizing his father and the other landowners and their peons. He posed as a lazy, foppish artistocrat, but secretly donned mask and sword to aid the oppressed.

Right: Roy Rogers and his horse, Trigger, were the stars on **The Roy Rogers Show** on NBC from 1951 to 1957, but they had able assistance from Dale Evans and Pat Brady. The cowboy star (born in Cincinnati) struck gold as the most popular television cowboy in the early 1950s–'The King of the Cowboys.' His themesong, written by his wife, Dale Evans, became a country classic–'Happy Trails to You.'

Opposite bottom: James Arness, as Matt Dillon, in a shootout on **Gunsmoke**.

Left: Will Hutchins played Tom 'Sugarfoot' Brewster on **Sugarfoot**, which ran on ABC from 1957 to 1961. It was the story of a young correspondence-school law student who went west to seek his fortune. Brewster turned out to be an exceedingly inept cowboy and was not even good enough to be called a tenderfoot, so he became 'Sugarfoot.' The show had a sense of humor and the hero ended up by capturing his share of outlaws—and pretty girls.

Opposite: Steve McQueen played bounty hunter Josh Randal in **Wanted: Dead or Alive**, a CBS program that ran from 1958 to 1961 on CBS. Randall wasn't big on the cowboy sixgun, preferring his 'Mare's Leg,' a cross between a hand gun and a rifle—a .30-40 sawed-off carbine that could be handled almost as easily as a pistol but had much more fire power. And Randall really knew how to handle it.

Left: Greg Palmer, shows engineer Allison Hayes the layout of mining property in an episode of **Death Valley Days**, the Western anthology that was syndicated from 1952 to 1975. It had several hosts—the most famous being Ronald Reagan (1965-66).

Above: James Drury was **The Virginian** on NBC from 1962 to 1971. Based on Owen Wister's 1902 novel, it told the story of the laconic, mysterious gunslinger who never revealed his real name, and was the first television Western to run for 90 minutes.

Left: **Rawhide** ran on CBS from 1959 to 1966 and gave most people their first glimpse of Clint Eastwood. Up to 1958 he had been able to pick up a few bit parts, usually in low-budget films. But he was photogenic, and the lightning struck when he was selected to play the second lead in **Rawhide**—as Rowdy Yates, the ramrod of the cattle drive. In this scene, Eastwood (left) and Sheb Wooley (as Pete Nolan, one of the trail hands) are being intimidated by guest villain Chester Morris. Much as **Wagon Train** took its characters west in their wagons, **Rawhide** took its characters, those men who organized and ran the communal cattle drives, east on their horses. Both shows told stories of the people and situations that they met along the way. Even the theme song, 'Rawhide,' written by Ned Washington and Dmitri Tiomkin and sung by Frankie Laine, became a hit.

Below: Eric Fleming (here shown with guest star Nina Foch) played the role of Gil Favor, the trail boss, on **Rawhide**. After Fleming died in an accidental drowning in 1966, Eastwood, as Rowdy Yates, took over the command of the cattle drive, organizing his own team to start another trek, but the show lasted only five more months.

Opposite: Ward Bond (left) was Major Seth Adams in **Wagon Train** and Robert Horton was Flint McCullough, his scout. The show appeared on NBC from 1957 to 1962, then switched to ABC from 1962 to 1966. Each season the California-bound wagon train would start to head west from St Joseph, Missouri and would reach California in the spring. Each week there were various adventures along the way on the Great Plains, the deserts and the Rocky Mountains. **Wagon Train** had two wagonmasters during its run. Bond was the first—the fatherly Major Adams. But Bond died after filming a few of the 1960-61 season's shows and was replaced by Chris Hale, played by John McIntire. Horton left the show in 1961 and was replaced by Scott Miller (as Duke Shannon), who was replaced by Robert Fuller (as Cooper Smith).

CHILDREN'S SHOWS

Almost from the beginning, children's programing has been an integral part of television. It probably began on the Dumont Network, where, in 1947 **The Small Fry Club** could be seen five times a week for a half an hour a day. Hosted by Bob Emery, it was a gentle show. Letters from kids would be read over the air; lessons on good behavior were taught; safety was discussed; children were told to drink more milk; a cast of actors would often do funny skits—dressed as different kinds of animals. Also in 1947, Dumont was offering **Birthday Party** for a half-hour on Thursdays. Over the years the hosts were Bill Slater, Aunt Grace and Ted 'King Kole' Brown, who worked with a group of talented kids who put on a birthday party for a different visiting child each week. Then in 1948 came the **Adventures of Oky Doky**, starring Oky Doky, a 30-inch tall mustachioed puppet, hosted by Wendy Barrie and Burt Hilber. Over the years, children's programing has proliferated—both in the area of entertainment and education. **Sesame Street** and others have done wonders in the field of entertainment; the Saturday cartoons are effective baby sitters; and the truly entertaining kid shows (**Kukla, Fran & Ollie, The Muppet Show**) can be adult favorites, too.

Above: Big Bird (created by Jim Henson) is one of the stars of **Sesame Street**—that wonderful Public Broadcasting System that has taught so many children to love learning by making it fun.
Left: A group of Henson characters—the Fraggles, who have appeared on pay television since 1983. Fraggles live in the caves of **Fraggle Rock**. One of the main characters is Uncle Matt, who likes to go exploring in 'outer space'—the human world beyond the Fraggle caves. Also on the show is Uncle Matt's nemesis, Sprocket the dog, and the lovable Doozers, who are cute little construction workers who are constantly building edifices that Fraggles like to munch on.
Opposite: The Muppet Show began on syndication in 1976, and 120 episodes were made. Here are Kermit the Frog (voice by Jim Henson) and Miss Piggy (voice by Frank Oz), the pig who wants to marry him. The show was a whimsical mixture of puppets and people.

Left: Kukla, Fran & Ollie ran on NBC from 1948 to 1952 and then on ABC from 1954 to 1957. Left to right: Kukla (meaning 'doll' in Russian), Burr Tillstrom (the creator of the Kuklapolitan Players), Fran Allison (the hostess) and Oliver J Dragon. Kukla was a kind, solemn, bulb-nosed little fellow with a perpetually astonished expression who knew nothing of his own past. Tillstrom was the creator, the voices and the puppeteer of all the Kuklapolitans. Allison was the hostess and the only human seen on the show. Ollie was a carefree and extroverted dragon who was born in Vermont where his parents ran Dragon Retreat. He was single-toothed and sentimental, had a terrible singing voice and couldn't breathe fire.

Above: A scene from **Kukla, Fran & Ollie** with Kukla (left) and Fletcher Rabbit at a lemonade stand. Fletcher was the mailman whose ears drooped so badly that they had to be starched for formal occasions. Others in the cast of Kuklapolitan puppets were Madam Ophelia Oglepuss, a haughty former opera star; Beulah Witch, who had studied electronics and rode her jet-propelled broom to patrol the coaxial cable; Cecil Bill, the strange-talking stage manager; Colonel Crackie, the long-winded Southerner who was master of ceremonies and also dated Beulah; Mercedes, the ingenue; Delores Dragon, the infant daughter of Ollie's Uncle Dorchester; and Olivia Dragon, Ollie's mother.

Above: Welcome to Pooh Corner was a four-part children's miniseries on the Disney Cable Channel. Based on the *Winnie The Pooh* books of A A Milne, it featured (left to right) Eeyore the donkey, Rabbit, Tigger the tiger, Owl, Winnie the Pooh (a bear) and, in front, Piglet.

Opposite bottom: Gentle, kind, intelligent Fred Rogers has been the host on **Mister Rogers' Neighborhood** on the Public Broadcasting System for more than 30 years. Here he is shown with a couple of his puppet friends. Rogers chats with his viewing audience in a charming, deliberate manner, subtly teaching them lessons in safety, behavior, nutrition and other important areas of knowledge. He also has guests on the program. The show is so much part of the American scene that one of Mr Rogers' sweaters is on display at the Smithsonian Institution.

Right: Marionette Howdy Doody with an admirer and Buffalo Bob Smith (who was also Howdy's voice). Perhaps no children's television program ever aquired as many loyal fans as **Howdy Doody**, which ran on NBC from 1947 to 1960. Beginning with Buffalo Bob's enthusiastic shout of 'Say, kids, what time is it?' and the resounding answer from the kids in the studio's 'Peanut Gallery' of **'It's Howdy Doody Time!!!**, the program was a zany melange of puppets, gadgets and live performers playing a variety of outrageous roles. Some of the supporting characters were Clarabelle the Clown (played by Bob Keeshan, who went on to win fame as **Captain Kangaroo**), Chief Thunderthud of the Ooragnak (spell it backwards) Indians (Bill Le Cornec), Princess Summerfall Winterspring (Judy Tyler) and Ugly Sam (Dayton Allen).

What would Saturday morning children's television be without top cartoon shows? Or, for that matter, what would late afternoon children's television be without cartoon shows? **The Small Fry Club** was running cartoons in 1947. Cartoons on television really got a shot in the arm in 1954 on ABC when **Walt Disney** began its 29-year run, often showing some of the Disney animated films. **The Flintstones**, that cartoon parody of modern suburban life set in the Stone Age, ran on ABC from 1960 to 1966. One spinoff was the Saturday morning show **Pebbles and Bamm Bamm**. Another spinoff was **The Jetsons**, a 21st century equivalent to **The Flintstones**, which ran on ABC from 1962 to 1963. **The Bullwinkle Show**, a spinoff of the ABC afternoon series **Rocky and His Friends** (1959-61), and featuring Bullwinkle J Moose and Rocky Squirrel, ran from 1961 to 1964 on NBC and then moved to ABC to run until 1973. These were just a few of the more popular cartoons shows,

Above: Yosemite Sam (left, dressed as an **Arabian Nights** character) and Bugs Bunny confront an irate child on **The Bugs Bunny Show,** which features the great old Warner Bros. cartoon shorts.
Left: Mickey Mouse, as a detective, is unaware of the ghost behind him. Mickey often appeared on the **Walt Disney** program and always on **The Mickey Mouse Club.**
Below left: Wile E Coyote, the nemesis of The Roadrunner, was a featured player in Warner Bros. cartoons that are often seen on television.
Below: The Flintstones. Standing left to right: Fred Flintstone, his wife Wilma, Barney Rubble, Dino (Fred's pet dinosaur) and Betty Rubble. Kneeling are Pebbles Flintstone and Bamm Bamm Rubble.

Left: Tom, the cat, and Jerry, the mouse, make up for a brief time in a **Tom and Jerry** cartoon from Metro-Goldwyn-Mayer. The series was a long-running one and Jerry was always able to outwit Tom, who tried every trick in the book to catch him. Jerry also danced with Gene Kelly in an imaginative scene in the movie **Anchors Aweigh** (1945).
Below left: A scene from **He-Man**. He-Man and She-Ra are standing in front of She-Ra's winged horse Stridor.
Below right: A scene from **The Transformers**—one of the better-drawn of the cartoon shows, and one that features children's toys.

Below: A scene from **A Charlie Brown Christmas** which featured Charles M Schulz, 'Peanuts' comic strip gang. This was the first of the more than a score of 'Peanuts' specials and appeared first on 9 December 1965 on CBS and won both an Emmy (best children's program) and a Peabody Award. The first showing drew more than 50 percent of the viewing audience in the United States.
Right: Inspector Gadget is a cartoon combination of Maxwell Smart and Inspector Clouseau.

Above: The 'Our Gang' movie shorts were always popular in the theaters and, rechristened **The Little Rascals**, they were rerun on television for years. Producer Hal Roach had originally gathered together a collection of child actors in the mid-1920s. They remained popular through the 1930s and 1940s, although the personnel of the team naturally changed. Roach had the idea that moviegoers would rather watch some plain kids who were up to ordinary mischief rather than a bunch of artificial stage brats. From the start, the key to its success was reality. The kids were believable and the studio had the sense to put them in fairly realistic situations. In the early 1930s, such future stars as Jackie Cooper, Dickie Moore and Scotty Beckett were members of the troupe, but Shirley Temple's application was turned down. Spanky

McFarland (left) was one of the mainstays of the gang, starting in 1932 and continuing for 11 years. He also played in feature films at the same time—**Kidnapped** (1934), **The Trail of the Lonesome Pine** (1936) and later in **Johnny Doughboy** (1943). Darryl Hickman (seated) was to go on to appear in many important films, such as **The Grapes of Wrath** (1940) and **Tea and Sympathy** (1954) and eventually to join brother Dwayne in **The Many Loves of Dobie Gillis** sitcom. Robert Blake (behind Hickman) appeared in many feature films, beginning with **Andy Hardy's Double Life** (1943, when he was nine years old), **The Treasure of the Sierra Madre** (1947—he was the Mexican boy who sold Humphrey Bogart the lottery ticket), **In Cold Blood** (1967) and **Tell Them Willy Boy Is Here** (1969).

Opposite below: Bob Keeshan (right) in a rather unusual costume for him. He played **Captain Kangaroo** for years on CBS dressed in a long coat of many pockets, out of which all manner of wonderful things were pulled to entertain his young audience. With him here is guest star Lou Jacobi, the veteran comedian. A regular on the show was Captain Kangaroo's friend, the farmer named Mr Greenjeans.

Right: In some ways, Soupy Sales was the kids' answer to Ernie Kovacs. The zany comedian got his first big break on local Detroit television, where he would mix gags with pies in the face. He was supported by White Fang, the nicest dog in the world, and Black Tooth, the meanest dog in the world (but only their paws were ever seen. He once got into a fair amount of trouble by telling his audience to send him 'those green pieces of paper from Daddy's wallet.'

Above: Over the years there were many replacements on **The Mickey Mouse Club**—here is a reunion of most of the mouseketeers.

Right The original Mouseketeers. Only Annette Funicello (center row far right) made it in show business.

Opposite top: The star of **Flipper** was a dolphin whose name was Suzy. She was the pet of 15-year-old Sandy Ricks (Luke Halpin) and his 10-year-old brother, Bud (Tommy Norden). They lived with their widowed father, Porter 'Po' Ricks (Brian Kelly), who was the chief ranger of Coral Key Park in Florida, in a cottage near the shore. The stories revolved around Flipper and his two young companions, with Bud involved more often than Sandy. The show ran on NBC from 1964 to 1967, and then come back from January to September of 1968. Andy Devine was also in the cast, playing an old marine carpenter.

Left: Lassie had a long and illustrious career, appearing on CBS from 1954 to 1971. She was always the brave, loyal, intelligent collie—alert and ever ready to help her masters and to protect them from adversity. Unfortunately, she was required to go through several sets of owners during her long tenure on television. In the beginning she lived with Jeff Miller (Tommy Rettig) his widowed mother, Ellen (Jan Clayton), and his grandfather, 'Gramps' Miller (George Cleveland) on a farm outside a town called Calverton. An orphan, Timmy (Jon Provost), joined them in 1957. George Cleveland died and the farm was sold to Paul and Ruth Martin (Hugh Reilly and June Lockhart), who kept Lassie and Timmy. In 1964 the Martins and Timmy went to Australia, leaving Lassie with Cully Wilson (Andy Clyde), who had a heart attack. Lassie went for help and found Ranger Corey Stuart (Robert Bray), with whom she moved in. After he was hurt, Lassie became a loner.

DOCTOR SHOWS

Television has always been filled with doctor shows—young doctors **(St Elsewhere)**, old doctors **(Marcus Welby)**, general practitioners **(The Practice)**, specialists **(Ben Casey)**. There have even been comedy shows about doctors **(The Bob Newhart Show, The Cosby Show)**. We never seem to get tired of these programs about sick people—perhaps they make us feel comfortable. It took them a while to get started—until 1952. That was the year in which **City Hospital**, starring Melville Ruick as Dr Barton Crane, and **The Doctor**, starring Warner Anderson in the title role, premiered. From then on, they bred like rabbits.

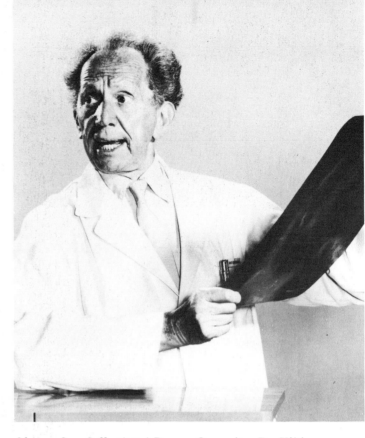

Above: Sam Jaffe played Dr David Zorba, the hero's mentor on **Ben Casey**. The show, which ran on ABC from 1961 to 1966, told of the surgeon, Casey (played by Vince Edwards), and his trials and tribulations with a succession of patients, most of whom seemed to have subdural haematomas. Jaffe left the program in 1965, and his position as resident wise man was taken over by Franchot Tone (as Dr Daniel Niles Freeland).

Left: Richard Chamberlain was Dr James Kildare in **Dr Kildare**, on NBC from 1961 to 1966.

Opposite: Dr Kildare kneeling, (center) renders emergency treatment to a traumatized patient. Kildare was a young intern and, as was the case with **Ben Casey** he had a medical father figure— Dr Leonard Gillespie (played by Raymond Massey). By the third season, the hero was promoted to resident. Kildare returned in a syndicated series, **Young Dr Kildare**, in 1972, starring Mark Jenkins as Kildare and Gary Merrill as Gillespie.

Below: Chad Everett played Dr Joe Gannon on **Medical Center**, which appeared on CBS from 1969 to 1976.

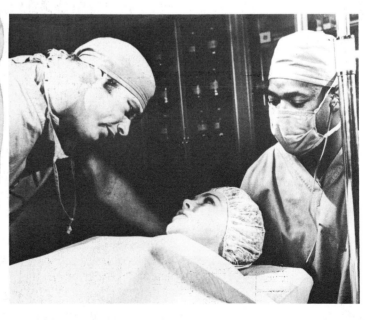

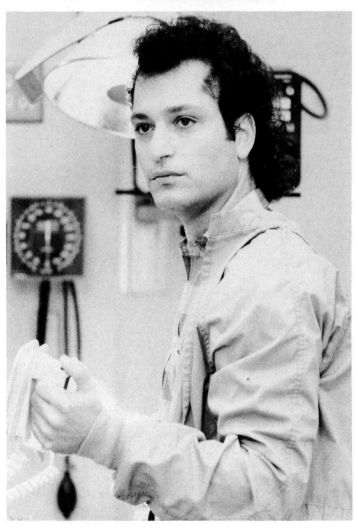

Above: Kindly Marcus Welby (Robert Young) comforts guest star Cloris Leachman in **Marcus Welby, M. D.**, the doctor show that ran on ABC from 1969 to 1976. The 62-year-old Young came out of a seven-year retirement (after **Father Knows Best**) to play in the series. Welby was a general practitioner in Santa Monica, California. The tension between youth and age was established when he took on a young assistant, Dr Steven Kiley (James Brolin), but it was Welby who was the more unorthodox of the two—often using a psychiatric approach to general practice. Welby had an exceedingly esoteric bunch of ailments to treat, especially for a GP. In the first season he had patients with tumors, autistic children, strokes, pernicious anemia, blindness, emphysema, LSD side effects, leukemia, diabetes, Huntington's Chorea, and dope addiction. He also treated a victim of faith healing, an overweight racing jockey and a diver who suffered from the bends. The show was number one in the ratings in 1970-71.

Right: An unusually grim Dr Wayne Fiscus (Howie Mandell) prepares to use defibrillator paddles in an attempt to jump-start the heart of a dying patient in **St Elsewhere**, which premiered on NBC in 1982. The main thing that made this show different from other medical dramas was the fact that there were no miracles. The physicians and surgeons were good, but sometimes the patient died. Also, the hospital, St Eligius, was the seediest ever seen on the television tube. Some of the situations were bizarre. Fiscus had an affair with a pathologist, Dr Cathy Martin (Barbara Whinnery), who insisted on making love on a slab in the morgue, among the sheet-draped corpses. Also in the cast were William Daniels (Dr Mark Craig), Ed Begley Jr (Dr Victor Erlich), David Morse (Dr Jack Morrison), Cynthia Sikes (Dr Annie Cavanero), Terence Knox (Dr Peter White) and Ellen Bry (Shirley Daniels, RN). In its first year, three of the actors won Emmys—Ed Flanders (who played Dr Donald Westphal) and guest stars Doris Roberts and James Coco.

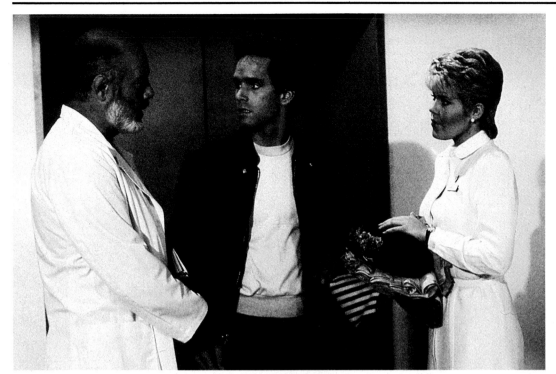

Left: Pernell Roberts (left) played **Trapper John M.D.**, the doctor show that premiered on CBS in 1979. It was a sort of spinoff from **M*A*S*H,** since the character of Dr John McIntyre had appeared in that show, set during the Korean War, and was played by Wayne Rogers.

Below: Robert Fuller (right) played Dr Kelly Brackett in **Emergency**, which ran on NBC from 1972 to 1977. It was a Jack Webb production, and so was done in his famous semi-documetary style, following the efforts of Squad 51 of the Los Angeles County Fire Department's Paramedical Rescue Service. Each episode depicted several interwoven incidents.

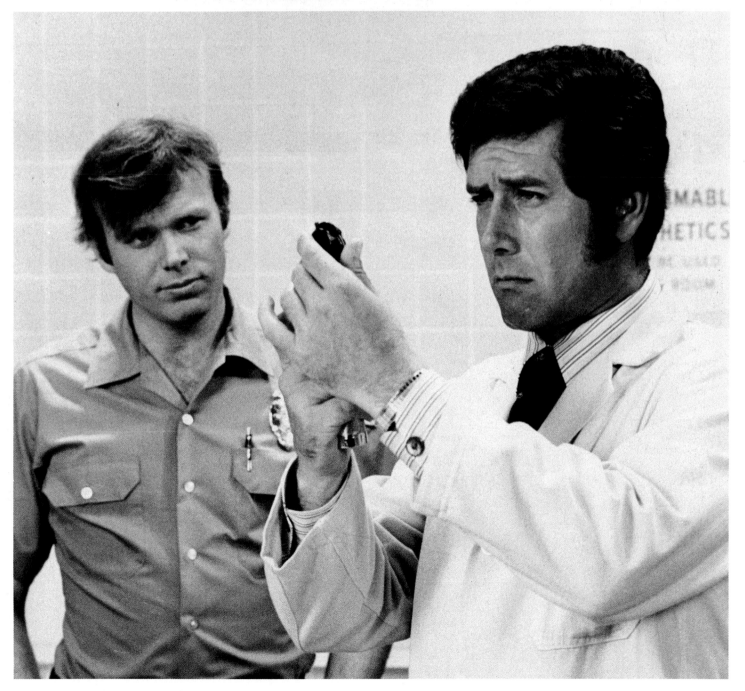

GAME SHOWS

Game shows have always been with us. Indeed, in network television's first year, 1946, the half-hour show **Play the Game** represented half of Dumont's Tuesday lineup. It was really a game of charades, pure and simple, and was hosted by an unlikely master of ceremonies—Dr Harvey Zorbaugh, a professor of educational sociology at New York University. Dumont came out with a similar show in 1947—**Charade Quiz**, hosted by Bill Slater. The charades were suggested by viewers and acted out by young actors in front of a panel of guessers. If the panel didn't guess the charade, the viewer who had sent it in won $15, which points up a reason why television networks love game shows. They are cheap to produce. More and more game shows appeared over the years. The first year of the big-money quiz show was 1955, when **The $64,000 Question** premiered on CBS. In 1956 came the spinoff **The $64,000 Challenge**, on which one contestant, Teddy Nadler won $252,000.

Left: Bob Barker with some of the gimmics used on **Truth Or Consequences**, a quiz show where contestants were asked silly questions which they almost always missed—therefore having to pay the consequences. It ran in prime time, in daytime, and in syndication for 28 years.

Above: Bill Cullen (left) was the host on **The Price Is Right**, in which contestants tried to guess the price of merchandise. It ran in prime time from 1957 to 1963 on NBC and from 1963 to 1964 on ABC.

Opposite: Dr Joyce Brothers hugs Eddie Egan (a former New York State Boxing Commissioner) on **The $64,000 Question** as host Hal March looks on. She had just won the top prize for answering questions on boxing.

Below: Garry Moore was the host of the daytime game show, **To Tell the Truth**, in which three contestants pretended to be the same person, answering questions put to them by a panel.

Above: Paul Lynde was the mainstay on **The Hollywood Squares**, a television version of tic-tac-toe, in which questions were asked of one of the nine celebrities stationed inside the squares of a tic-tac-toe board. The contestants would then have to state whether the answer was right or wrong. Three X's or O's in a row won the game.

Below: Richard Dawson (in the foreground) was the host on **Family Feud**, which premiered in 1977. Two families of five members each were presented with questions such as 'name the month when a pregnant woman begins to show.' The correct answers had previously been determined by a survey. The family with the most points won.

Above: Chuck Barris was the producer and for four years the master of ceremonies on **The Gong Show,** a syndicated program that was produced from 1976 to 1980. It was a parody of the old amateur hour shows on radio. Most of the contestants were cerified crazies—people who whistled through their noses, a dentist who could play songs on his drill, fat ladies who tap danced, a comedian who performed inside a barrel. They were graded (or gonged) by members of a panel of funny people, among them, from time to time, were Jay P Morgan, Jamie Farr, Rex Reed, Phyllis Diller, Arte Johnson and Rip Taylor. Another guest was 'The Unknown Comic,' who told terrible jokes while wearing a bag over his head. One critic called the show 'A cuckoo's nest without walls.'
Opposite: Bob Eubanks was the host on **The Newlywed Game,** another Chuck Barris production, which ran in prime time on ABC from 1967 to 1971 in daytime (1966-74) and on syndication.

NEWS

Probably the oldest genre of television programming is the news show. Indeed, NBC was telecasting the news on its experimental local New York station in 1939, and hired superstar Lowell Thomas to do the program in 1940. Also on NBC, William Spargrove was on weekly as the **Esso Television Reporter** in 1940 and Sam Cuff appeared on **Face of the War** from 1941 to 1942. Dumont began its news coverage in 1947 with **Walter Compton News**, originating in Washington, DC. ABC began in 1948 with **News and Views**, co-anchored by H R Baukhage and Jim Gibbons. CBS also started in 1948 with a news show anchored by Douglas Edwards—who was to stay with the program for 14 years. Probably the most ambitious undertaking in television news in recent years was Ted Turner's Cable News Network. CNN started broadcasting 24 hours of news in 1982 and has had a great impact on the industry. It not only competes with the networks itself, it furnishes remotes to independent stations, thus making their local newscasts more competitive.

Above: Edward R Murrow was the dean of television newsmen. He was given an Emmy in 1954 for being the Most Oustanding Personality in television, and was given an Emmy for Best News Commentator in 1956, 1957, 1958 and 1959. His **See It Now** program was the prototype of quality television documentary shows. He also hosted **Small World** and **Person to Person**.

Above: A young Walter Cronkite hosted **You Are There** in 1953. The subject of the program was the **Hindenburg** Disaster in 1937. Cronkite took over the CBS anchor desk from Douglas Edwards on 16 April 1962, staying there until 6 March 1981. He had spent almost two decades coming into our living rooms five days a week and his soft-spoken voice of authority had made him an institution.

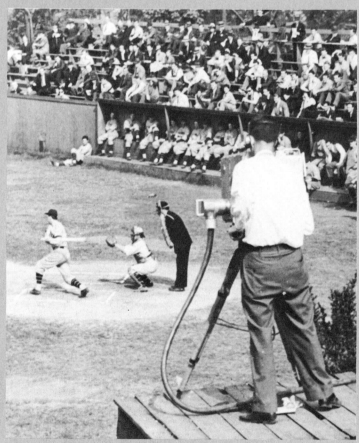

Above: The first television coverage of a baseball game was aired on 17 May 1939. It was at Baker Field in New York City and pitted Princeton University against the home team—Columbia University. Later in the year, Red Barber would be the announcer of another NBC baseball game at Brooklyn's Ebbetts Field between the Dodgers and the Reds.

Above: Walter Winchell had long been a gossipy newsman in the press and on radio, and he made the switch to television easily. **The Walter Winchell Show** of news and commentary ran on ABC from 1952 to 1955 and for two months in 1960. Then came a variety show, also called **The Walter Winchell Show**, on NBC in 1956. There was also **The Walter Winchell File**, a crime anthology that ran on ABC from 1957 to 1958. Winchell was also famous for being the narrator on **The Untouchables** from 1959 to 1963 on ABC. The show had started out as a two-episode play on CBS's **Westinghouse Desilu Playhouse** on 20 and 27 April 1959, with Winchell as narrator, and Robert Stack as Eliot Ness.

Right: Senator Joseph McCarthy of Wisconsin, the chairman of a Senate subcommittee in 1952 exhibiting 'evidence' of Communist activities. It was television that unseated this character assassin. He was exposed in 1954 on the telecasts of the Army-McCarthy hearings and censured by the Senate.

Left: The television coverage of the Kefauver hearings was so spectacular that this New York movie theater dropped its regular Hollywood fare to show them on its screen. The interest in these hearings was the result of television editorial direction, coloring what would otherwise have been a purely impartial piece of news coverage, which came at the request of the victim during Senator Estes Kefauver's Senate Crime Hearings in the 1950s. Witness Frank Costello, a mobster, asked the senator from Tennessee that his face not be shown on television. The television director obliged, and had his cameras pointed at Costello's nervous, sweaty hands during the tough questioning. Millions of viewers focused on these guilt-covered hands and also on Kefauver. Indeed, Kefauver gained so much fame and believability from these television shows that he made a run for the Democratic Party's nomination for president. He campaigned wearing a Davy Crockett coon-skin hat, and almost made it.

Right: For the first time in history, the nominees of the Republican and Democratic parties debated on television. The moderator of the debate, seated on the dais between John F Kennedy and Richard M Nixon, was Howard K Smith of ABC. The first of the four hour-long nationally televised debates between Nixon and Kennedy took place in Chicago. The viewers' complaints that Nixon looked haggard and drawn made television an issue in the campaign. Actually he could, indeed, have used a better makeup man, since he also looked unshaven. Many observers felt that the debates helped Kennedy's cause by giving him a wider audience and demolishing Republican arguments on his immaturity. Others felt that Nixon's participation was the biggest single factor leading to his defeat. Whatever the after effects, this was a historic confrontation, and one that has been repeated many times in national election campaigns.

Above: Television was there in Dallas when President John F Kennedy was assassinated on 22 November 1963. This shot was made just about one minute before the rifle was fired. Also in the car are Jacqueline Kennedy and Governor and Mrs John Connally of Texas. A stunned nation followed the tragedy and its aftermath on television—including the fatal shooting of accused assassin Lee Harvey Oswald by night club owner Jack Ruby during a jail transfer two days later. Kennedy was buried in Arlington National Cemetery with full military honors.
Left: Television has always covered the comings and goings of presidents. Here Richard M Nixon boards the presidential helicopter after his resignation 9 August 1974. After his private tapes were made known to the American public, it was learned that he had lied about the Watergate affair, and, threatened with impeachment, he wisely chose to resign.

Opposite: In the late 1940s and early 1950s, newscaster John Cameron Swayze presided over the **Camel News Caravan** on NBC. Critics called it 'the most interesting and authoritative news program on television.'

Left: Dave Garroway (right), the original host of NBC's **Today Show**, which began broadcasting in 1952, with producer James Fleming
Below: Robert MacNeill and Jim Lehrer are the hosts of the award-winning **MacNeill/Lehrer Newshour** on PBS.

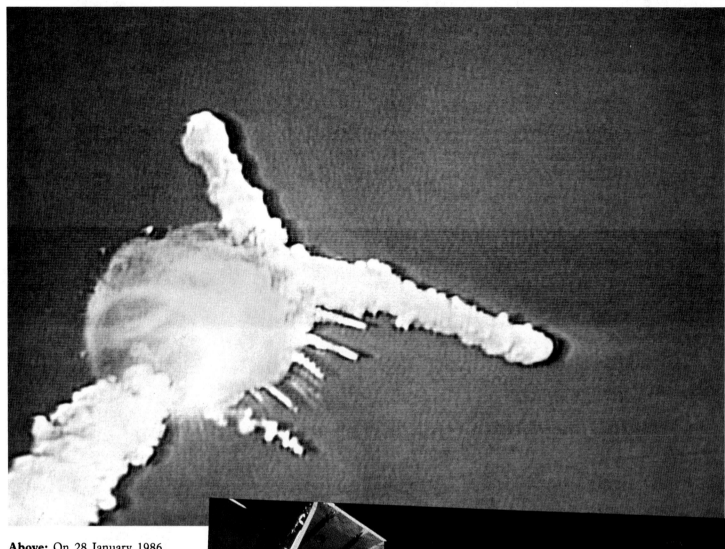

Above: On 28 January 1986, the space shuttle **Challenger** lifted off from Cape Canaveral with its crew of seven aboard. Space launches had become so common that only CNN—the Cable News Network—was covering the story. Seventy-three seconds later, millions of television viewers saw the tragic explosion that took the lives of Christa McAuliffe, a New Hampshire school teacher who was to have been the first civilian in space; Francis R Scobee, the commander of **Challenger;** Judith Resnik, a NASA astronaut; Ronald McNair, a black astronaut with a doctorate in physics; Michael Smith, a pilot-astronaut; Ellison Onizuka, an astronaut who was a former test pilot for the Air Force; and Gregory Jarvis, a satellite engineer, who was also trained as an astronaut.

Right: The first moon walk was covered by television via satellite. It was made by Neil A Armstrong, who was a member of the crew of the Apollo-Saturn 11 mission which blasted off on 16 July 1969 and returned 24 July.

INDEX

PHOTO CREDITS

The Bettman Archive: 16 (bottom), 21 (bottom left), 23, 4 (bottom), 28 (bottom), 30 (top), 32 (bottom), 33-34, 35, 40 (top), 51 (top), 58 (bottom left), 94 (bottom), 132 (top right), 133, 136 (bottom left and right), 140, 141 (top)

Bison Photo Library: 4-5, 8, 11 (bottom), 12, 15, 20 (left), 21 (bottom right), 31, 32 (top), 34 (bottom right), 38, 40 (bottom right and left), 41 (top), 42 (top), 43 (top), 45 (bottom), 46 (bottom), 47 (center), 48 (bottom), 49, 50 (top), 50-51, 51 (bottom), 55 (bottom), 60 (top right), 62-63, 64-65, 66 (top), 69 (top and bottom right), 70, 71 (bottom), 76 (top), 77 (top right), 78 (bottom), 88 (bottom), 91 (top), 92 (bottom), 93 (bottom), 94 (top), 95 (top), 96, 97 (top), 102, 103 (bottom), 106, 107 (bottom), 108-109, 112 (top), 124 (top), 127 (bottom), 128 (bottom right), 129, 138 (top and bottom), 139 (top and bottom).

Granada Television 95 (bottom).

Rick Marschall: 79, 81 (bottom), 86, 87 (top left and bottom), 89 (top), 92 (top).

Museum of Modern Art Film Stills Archives: 22-23, 120 (center). NASA: 142.

National Film Archives: 60 (top left), 61, 128 (left).

Peter Newark's Western Americana: 137 (bottom). Don Perdue: 141 (bottom).

Phototeque: 13 (center), 16 (top), 20-21, 24 (top left), 26 (left), 27-28 (bottom), 28 (top), 36 (bottom), 37 (top), 60 (bottom), 74 (bottom), 75, 103 (top), 104 (top), 105 (bottom right), 109 (bottom), 125, 132 (left and bottom right), 137 (top).

Rogers: 2 (lower right), 3 (left), 9 (bottom left and right), 10, 11 (top), 13 (top and bottom), 14, 16 (center), 17, 18, 19, 24 (top right), 25, 26-27 (top), 28, 29, 30 (bottom), 34 (top and bottom), 35, 36 (top), 37 (bottom), 39, 41 (bottom), 42 (bottom), 43 (bottom), 44 (bottom), 45 (top), 46 (top right and left), 47 (top and bottom left and right), 48 (top), 50 (bottom left), 52, 53, 54, 55 (top), 58-59, 59, 62, 66 (bottom), 67, 68, 69 (bottom left), 71 (top), 72, 73, 74 (top), 76 (bottom), 77 (top left and bottom), 78 (top), 80, 81 (top), 82, 83, 87 (top right), 88 (top), 89 (bottom), 90, 91 (bottom), 93 (bottom), 97 (bottom), 98, 99, 100, 101, 104 (bottom), 105 (top and bottom left), 107 (top), 108 (bottom), 110, 111, 112 (bottom), 113, 114, 115, 116, 117, 118, 119, 120 (top and bottom), 121, 122, 123, 124 (Bottom), 126, 127 (top), 128 (top right), 130, 131, 134, 135, 136 (top),

The author and publisher would like to thank the following people wbo have helped in the preparation of this book: Mike Rose, who designed it; Elizabeth Montgomery, who edited it; Mary R Raho and Donna Cornell, who did the picture research and Cynthia Klein who prepared the index.